On Edward Hicks

BY SANFORD SCHWARTZ

The Art Presence

Artists and Writers

Christen Købke

William Nicholson

On Edward Hicks

Sanford Schwartz

Lucia | Marquand, Seattle

Library of Congress Cataloging-in-Publication Data

Names: Schwartz, Sanford, 1946– author.
Title: On Edward Hicks / Sanford Schwartz.
Description: Seattle : Lucia|Marquand, [2021] | Includes bibliographical references and index.
Identifiers: LCCN 2020030010 | ISBN 9781646570065 (hardback)
Subjects: LCSH: Hicks, Edward, 1780–1849—Criticism and interpretation.
Classification: LCC ND237.H58 S39 2021 | DDC 759.13—dc23
LC record available at https://lccn.loc.gov/2020030010

Published by Lucia|Marquand, Seattle
www.luciamarquand.com

Available through:
ARTBOOK | D.A.P.
75 Broad Street, Suite 630
New York, NY 10004
www.artbook.com

Jacket: Edward Hicks, *Peaceable Kingdom* (c. 1830–32), oil on canvas, 17 ⅞ × 23 ⅞ in. (45.5 × 60.6 cm), detail. The Metropolitan Museum of Art, New York, NY; gift of Edgar William and Bernice Chrysler Garbisch, 1970.

Contents

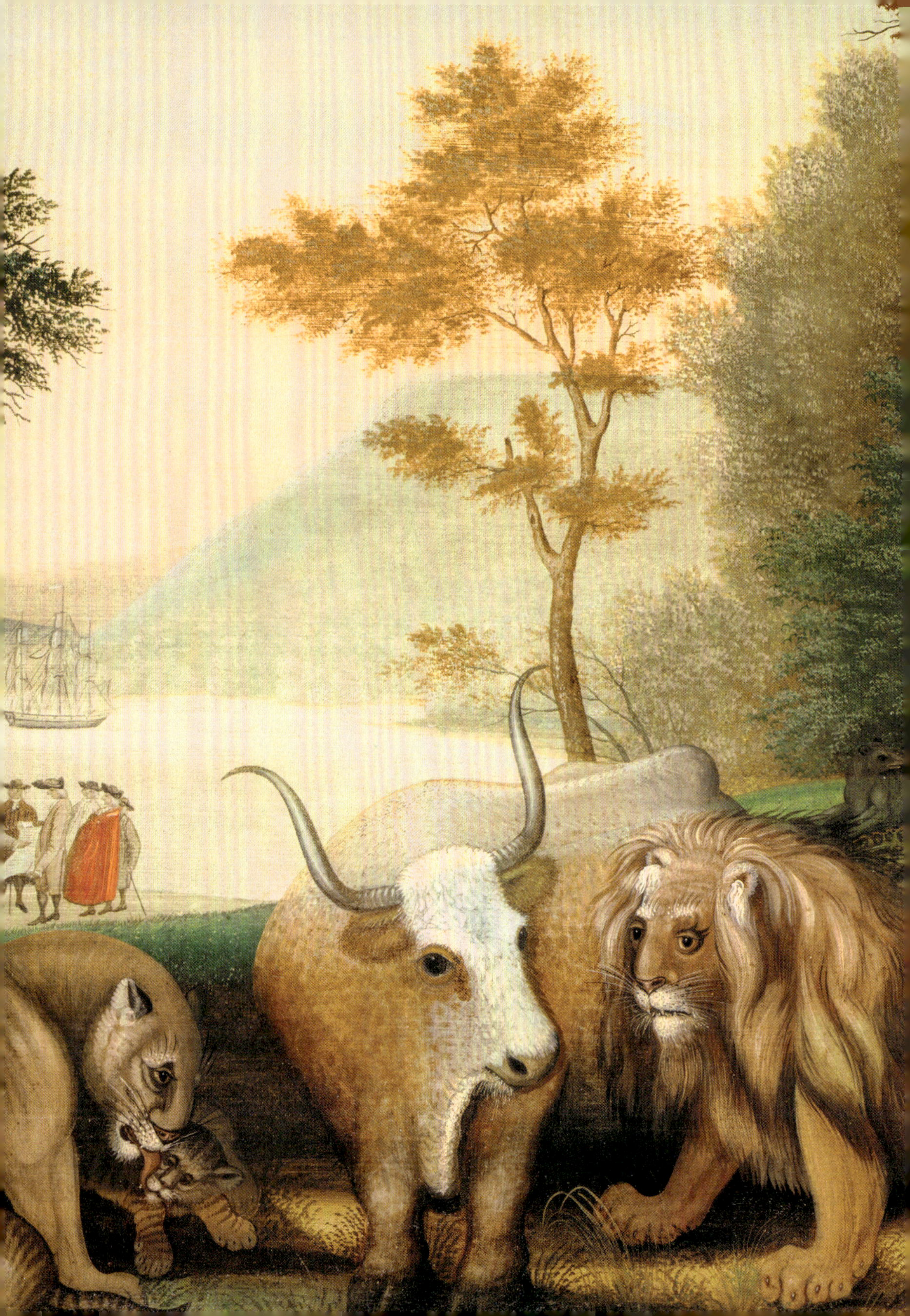

Preface

Edward Hicks would probably say that his continuing invisibility in the history of art—his being, as a friend who is an art critic noted, little more than a "cipher" even in the annals of American art—made perfect sense. A Quaker minister who was fervent about his religion and whose religion frowned on the practice of most arts, Hicks virtually never put himself forward as an artist. He was proud not to do so. He barely mentioned his even being a painter in his extensive autobiographical writings, and he never publicly noted that he was the author of the linked group of works called *Peaceable Kingdom*, surely one of the most remarkable series of paintings in the art of any era. Needless to say, Hicks drew scant attention, either, to his paintings of farms, a subject that few American artists handled with equal depth, and the Quaker minister was, naturally, largely silent about any other kinds of pictures he made.

When Hicks died, in 1849, at sixty-nine, more people attended his funeral, in Newtown, Pennsylvania, than the region had ever witnessed on such an occasion. The three to four thousand people who came that late summer day, likely jamming the narrow streets of the colonial-era town, were there primarily because of Hicks's renown as a preacher. Some of those in attendance likely knew that the man supported himself and his family as a commercial painter, a decorator of carriages and of the many wood household objects that in the days before industrialization called out for a little ornamentation. But that Edward also made easel paintings would not have been widely known at all.

As the creator of *Peaceable Kingdom*—the realm where beasts of prey commingle with the defenseless creatures they would normally devour—Hicks has long been a beckoning, if also, by his own design, largely intangible, figure. I tried to write about Alice Ford's coffee-table-style biography of him when it came out in 1985 and had to forego the possibility, in good part because, while loaded with information, *Edward Hicks: His Life and Art* was resolutely local in spirit. Although his pictures were described, the descriptions were lost in the many details about Hicks and his family connections, his Quakerism, the stresses that the religion went through in those days, and the sources for his pictures. What I now see was missing was how these details might have mattered in the larger life of art. The same issue besets Ford's much finer *Edward Hicks: The Painter of the Peaceable Kingdom*, from 1952, which remains the definitive biography.

In recent years, though, as I visited many museums with the thought of writing an informal guide to nineteenth-century American painting, Hicks finally came into focus. I had never looked at his Kingdoms in relation to other artworks, and, despite Ford's writing and the illustrations in her book, I had not realized so clearly that Hicks kept rethinking the appearance and spirit of his Kingdoms—and that in their entirety they could be seen as presenting a single large story and were, too, similar to a notebook in which he tested different approaches. As I kept going to see works by Winslow Homer, Thomas Cole, Mary Cassatt, John F. Peto, and the rest, I came to tailor these trips to collections that included Hicks, and in due time he elbowed his way to the foreground of my study. Then he elbowed everyone else out.

As I attempted to take the measure of Hicks and how he related to his contemporaries, I learned that contradictoriness is built into almost every aspect of the man and his work. That many museumgoers in America have heard of his name and can picture a *Peaceable Kingdom* in their minds, and at the same moment have no idea who Hicks is, is one such contradiction. I came to see as well that while he is routinely labeled our foremost folk artist, his Kingdoms stretch the idea of folk art so greatly as to be almost a misnomer. The subtlest contradiction has to do with what he meant by "peaceable." His images of the lion, the leopard, and the other wild, rapacious creatures, who have come together for the moment with the ox, the sheep, and the other tame and retiring animals, are on one level statements of a Quaker's pacifist convictions. But the creaturely cast of the Kingdoms can make us forget that we are looking at visualized sermons; or as Joan Acocella put it, writing about Reynard the Fox, "Animal narratives have allowed writers with lessons on their mind to make art rather than just lessons."

In the pages that follow, I have tried to present how, much as he was a minister who happened to make oil paintings, Hicks was also an imaginative creator who was a minister. This is an unorthodox view in the writing on him, and he might have chafed at the thought. But the evidence of his paintings, I believe, says it is so. His richest ones include, in addition to numerous *Peaceable Kingdoms*, farm scenes of great breadth and—also from the latter half of the 1840s, his last years—a resplendent painting of Noah's Ark. Taken together, they are works that at times have a Neoclassical poise, and in other instances display a stormy Baroque exuberance—or, more typically, a feeling for the mysteries of forest life that recall the contemporaneous work of the Brothers Grimm. Whether or not they are labeled folk art, they are among the high points of American art.

My aim is not to cover exhaustively Hicks's life as a painter, a Quaker, or a person, but, rather, to suggest—in chapters that pick up his story from different angles—ways in which he was a monumental, and hard to compartmentalize, figure. He might be pleased to know that the power and energy he exerted as a minister, attested to by the many people who attended his funeral, remain undimmed in his work as an artist.

My thanks go to the Hicks scholars who paved the way for me and whose names appear throughout the text; and to Eve Bowen, Tom Bishop, Adrian Lucia and his staff at Lucia | Marquand, Laura Pass Barry, James Callahan, Sharon Horvath, Carroll Janis, Michael Steger, James Barron, and, for their special efforts, Nick Weber and Jeffrey Hoffeld. My gratitude goes to Jeanette Sisk, who addressed countless issues over a long time with confidence and unfailing grace, to Eugenia Bell, whose scrupulous and friendly eye made the manuscript fit to leave home, and to Tom Eykemans, whose design ideas gave me the book I hoped for. *On Edward Hicks*, lastly, would not have happened without the mind and spirit of Carole Obedin.

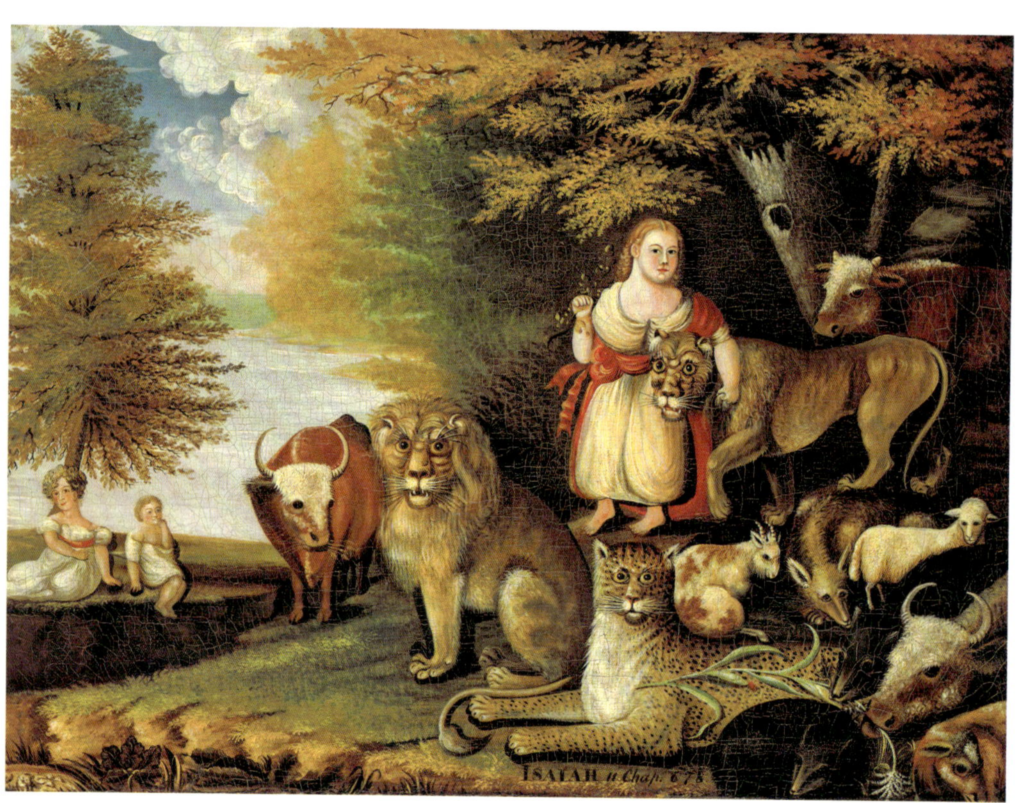

Edward Hicks, *Peaceable Kingdom*, c. 1830–32, 17 7⁄8 × 23 7⁄8 in. (45.5 × 60.6 cm).

An Outdoor Living Room

PRESENTING A DREAM of friendliness and serenity yet often tense and unsettling—and starring, as it were, an almost all-animal cast yet clearly about human experience—Edward Hicks's many paintings entitled *Peaceable Kingdom* might be called inside-out masterpieces. In pictures set at the edge of a wood, we see an assembly of wild beasts, including a bear and a wolf, and of tame, or farm, animals, including a kid and a cow. They are living as a group, as the words "peaceable kingdom" would suggest, in a domain where predators and their prey have come to coexist.

But the scenes, where the animals are often jumbled together, seem as much to show a peace conference that has only just gotten underway after a recent ceasefire. Harmony is less in the air than something unexpectedly realistic and psychological. We scan the faces and bodies of the animals and find a mixture of good intentions and sleepy indifference, arrogant self-importance, and some wariness—while for the leopard this convening often seems to be no more than a chance to preen for attention.

• • •

FEW ARTWORKS BY an American are as immediately and as widely recognizable as the *Peaceable Kingdoms*. And whether it is an accurate estimate or not, probably no other artworks connote the spirit of American folk art as readily. A detail of even a few of the preemptory, edgy, or merely adorable creatures found in these pictures can make people believe that they have landed in the center of folk art's presumably innocent-hearted and sometimes unwittingly bizarre realm. Done over a thirty-year period from about the early 1820s through the 1840s, they all have roughly the same structure. The animals are accompanied by a child, who in some of the early pictures is the principal figure. Off in the distance, the scene opens out to a watery and brighter expanse, where, in many of the pictures, people stand on the shore and sometimes a sailing ship is in view.

Some sixty versions of the scene have come to light, and that Hicks made so many paintings of the same image over the years may be as memorable to viewers as the scene itself. This repetitiousness would seem to be a sign of the innate industriousness we often ascribe to naive painters. And at times, it is true, he repeated himself so closely he was nearly making replicas.

But Hicks periodically made shifts in how he grouped his creatures and what moods they were expressing. He changed the roles the different animals played, and he rearranged the light and atmosphere of the setting; and seeing in one gallery, on their own, almost any ten or a dozen Kingdoms chosen from different times would make for one of the singular joys of painting, American or otherwise. It would be like seeing a fairy-tale realm through the eyes of an artist who focuses our minds by subtly altering the same image on different canvases. And the more Kingdoms we take in, the harder it is to make blanket declarations of what they are about.

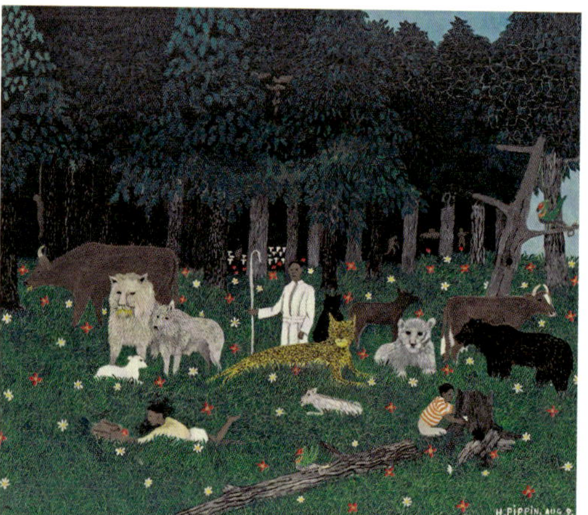

Horace Pippin, *The Holy Mountain III*, 1945, 25 1/4 × 30 1/4 in. (64.6 × 76.8 cm).

As calls for a cessation of hostilities, Hicks's paintings have an underlying moral strength; they are ethical and social injunctions. They stem from a prophesy in Isaiah 11:6–9. The prophet is talking about a coming time of "righteousness" when natural antagonisms will be suspended, and carnivores and vegetarians, or the killers and the innocent, will come together. The lion will "eat straw like the ox," and the "leopard will lie down with the kid." The wolf will "dwell with the lamb" and the bear and the cow will "feed" together. Isaiah includes, as well, the offspring of some of these creatures, and says that "a little child shall lead them." He concludes his group with a "suckling" and a "weaned" child, each putting a hand in or on an opening in the earth where a poisonous creature dwells. It is only in the ninth verse that he makes his dream explicit when he says, "They shall not hurt nor destroy in all my holy mountain . . ."

While some are familiar with this Biblical passage, it was rarely taken up by artists of any time or nation before Hicks. The theme, and Hicks's precedent, did, however, inspire a painter a century later. This was Horace Pippin—whose dealer, Robert Carlen, of Philadelphia, also handled works by Hicks—who, between 1944 and 1946, made three versions of the Old Testament verses (and left an unfinished one), setting the scene in a summertime field. And in recent years Sharon Horvath, whose paintings are largely abstract, was drawn to the way the *Peaceable Kingdoms*, though done slightly before Charles Darwin and our modern understanding of evolution, are a display of this kind of change. About her series based on the Kingdoms, she wrote, "As an homage, I revisited and let myself be imprinted by Hicks's compositions, playing with and, I like to think, extending their evolution into this century."

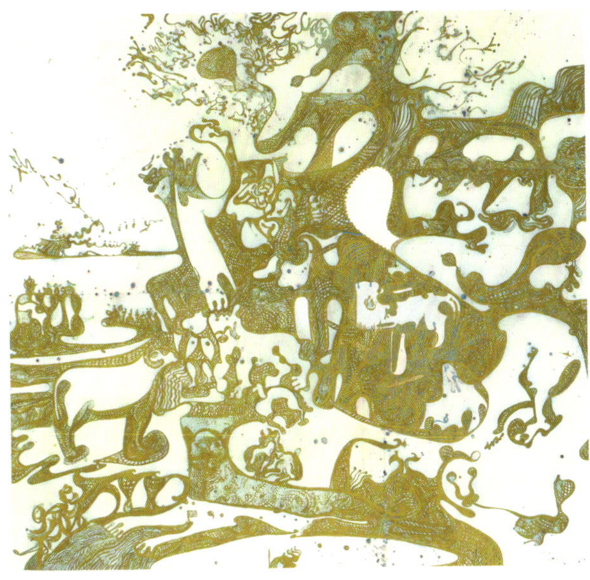

Sharon Horvath, *Peaceable (for Edward Hicks)*, 2008, 48 × 52 ½ in. (121.9 × 133.3 cm).

Isaiah's are words that Hicks, who lived in an era of acrimonious discord among his fellow Quakers, took seriously. It has been thought that his wanting to make pictures of the muting of factionalism stemmed from his heightened awareness of the way the Society of Friends, in the 1820s, was being rent by members wanting Quaker observance to go in one direction or its opposite. It was an altercation serious enough to result in the Separation of 1827. Yet Hicks was driven to the prophesy as well through a lifelong personal need—an almost therapeutic need—to atone for or to keep in check his own emotional flare-ups and animosities. His *Peaceable Kingdoms* thus have the fiber of sermons, of social commentary, and of a personal quest. What has given them their life, though, is that they also have the appeal and mystery of fables. Their origins in religion don't have to be factors in the pleasure we take from them. If my son's response to the Kingdoms at age ten is typical—we were at the last large Hicks show, which traveled to the Philadelphia Museum of Art in 2000—they are pictures that children know were made for adults but can feel were also created with them in mind.

Painted by a craftsman whose commercial assignments were meant to weather the elements, Hicks's Kingdoms appear much as they must have to their earliest viewers. The surfaces of the pictures might today exhibit craquelure, but their colors remain bright and clear. Hicks's coloring can be monotonous. He was after all repeating the same scene. But he could adroitly bring together assertive, full-bodied greens, reds, oranges, and blues—his employment of so many fundamental colors at once can remind us of our first boxes of Crayola—and there are delectable touches of white on many of the animals.

The wolf, with his distancing, stylized face and bony, angular, jangling body, is made up of markings in white and gray—markings that make him recall a Pacific Northwest Indigenous carving. The liver-red ox often sports a dramatic curving white line along the ridge of his back and another down his chest. And the pictures have a breathing life when seen close-up. Applying oil paint with brusqueness and confidence, Hicks gets the leopard's fur, for instance, to have the very texture of fur and also to look, appealingly, like strokes of a brush.

The surrounding trees and leaves, and the light that seeps through them, are such strong presences as to make the Kingdoms sometimes feel like landscapes that happen to include figures. In his ledger, Hicks did refer to "landscapes" he made, but these mentions are rare and it isn't clear what the pictures are of. In his Kingdoms he was certainly effective in conveying the white heat of a summer's day, and he was even finer with the red, orange, yellow, and brown tones, and the warming pink skies of autumn. One of the more alluring aspects of the setting is how Hicks, who rarely presents more than a handful of trees, suggests that the animals are emanating from, or slipping back into, a deep, dark wood.

He gives us a kind of romance of the forest, and in this, and in the way the creatures form a floating inventory of animal life, *Peaceable Kingdoms* are like distant relatives of one of the most marvelous of all paintings that feature animals, Pisanello's *Vision of Saint Eustace* (not that Hicks had necessarily heard of the Renaissance artist). In this early fifteenth-century (and much reworked) picture, a young, princely figure on horseback has encountered a stag in a forest, and between the stag's horns a crucifix has materialized. But the picture tells a related story in its enveloping terrain of ravines and ledges, which provides just the right customized showcases for the many birds, deer, and sniffing dogs—and the bounding hare and the bear—that we see.

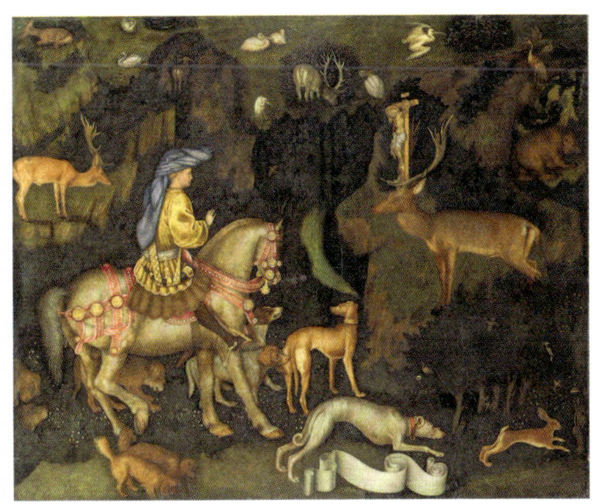

Pisanello, *The Vision of Saint Eustace*, c. 1438–42, 21 1/2 × 25 3/4 in. (54.8 × 65.5 cm).

Hicks's Kingdoms and Pisanello's panel are paintings about religious experience made by artists whose instinctive love seems to be the spirit and shape of animals. The painters, as it happens, present terrain in exactly the same way—as grass-topped "eroded rims of earth" (as Alice Ford described it). And like Pisanello, Hicks, with his mystic awareness on the one hand and his grasp, on the other, of the natural world at its most elegant, gives us two realms at once. There is the sprawling assembly of Isaiah's animals and children and then, in the back, on the shore, a tiny drama is underway.

The event might show William Penn, the seventeenth-century Quaker who was a hero to Hicks, entering into his famous treaty with the local

Lenni Lenape Indians—in actuality Penn conducted more a meeting than a treaty signing—or the figures we see might be a group of Quakers. These diminutive people are not arresting in themselves, but their mere presence adds a formal and expressive tension to the Kingdoms. We assume the faraway historical figures represent "reality," or are figments of some historical reality, and that the animals and children are a "vision." But what we feel, amusingly and disorientingly, is the opposite.

• • •

HICKS IS AT his most powerful, however, as a delineator of character and emotion. The Kingdoms have not been written about as such, but they can be viewed as a kind of genre scene or group portrait. We could be looking at an outdoor living room. It is a scene where, taking in Hicks's different versions, a single family has come together year after year, rather like the way, in projects undertaken by photographers or movie directors, we return to the same siblings, grade school class, or people living in the same place and chart the changes—as Ingmar Bergman, looking at an island in the Baltic, did in the films *Fårö Document* (1970) and *Fårö Document 1979*.

Encountering a *Peaceable Kingdom,* we tend to look first at the lion, and while he is not always the central character, he sets the tone of the whole. His physical presence is often a surprise. His legs and paws can have the monumental sturdiness of a carousel animal, and his powerful muscularity makes one realize how much each Kingdom is a collection of distinctive, self-contained shapes. But it is his spirit that

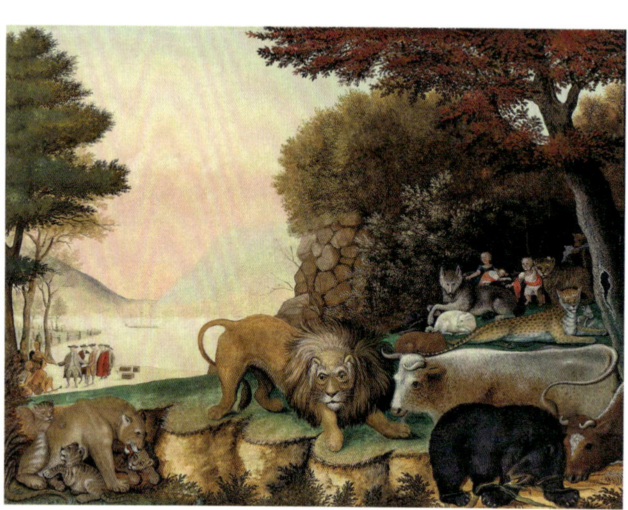

Edward Hicks, *Peaceable Kingdom,* 1846–47, 26 × 32 1/2 in. (64.5 × 82.5 cm).

draws us in. From one Kingdom to the next he exhibits a fierce pride—or angered dissatisfaction. He might show a startled vigilance, or a benevolent, even wearied sagacity.

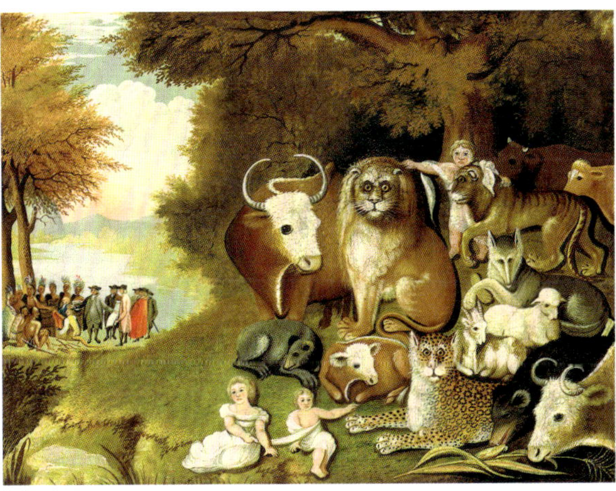

Edward Hicks, *Peaceable Kingdom*, c. 1833, 17 7⁄8 × 23 15⁄16 in. (45.4 × 60.8 cm).

The very fine commentator on Hicks, Eleanore Price Mather, has perceptively written that, in a Kingdom from 1847 where the lion appears lost and bewildered, and stands none too sturdily by himself on the grassy stage, he recalls King Lear. One might add that in other Kingdoms, where the lion sits on his haunches and appears nervous, bug-eyed, and guilty-looking, he recalls, as well, Macbeth.

Gradually, however, we wonder whether the leopard isn't stealing the show from the lion. Sometimes the leopard is so stretched out that he resembles a carpet runner. Or, on his feet and with his back arched and his mouth wide open, he is plain frightening. He seems to have in him the wildness, unpredictability, and cruelty that is only dimly there in the bear and the wolf and that we lose sight of in the lion—who, after a while, doesn't seem like an animal at all but, put simply, a very expressive being. The leopard is always an animal, and unfathomable. His physical elasticity and changeability make him forever suspect.

The ox, on the other hand, is immobile—and, increasingly as Hicks made these pictures, huge as a house. He is less a character than an invaluable presence. He sometimes has the deepest and loveliest eyes of any of the creatures, though his eyes, unlike those of

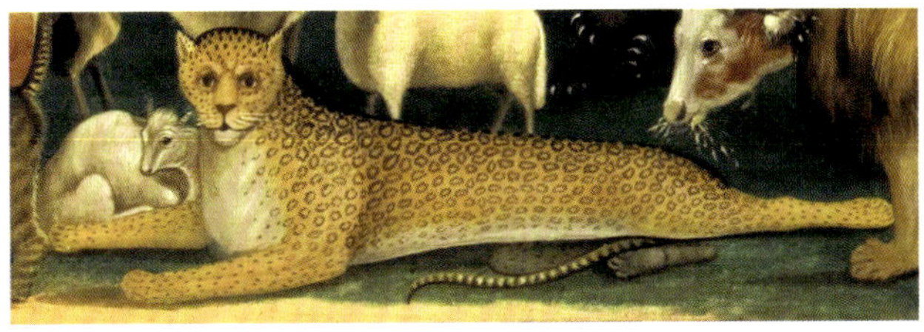

Edward Hicks, *Peaceable Kingdom*, c. 1849, 24 × 30 1⁄4 in. (60.9 × 76.8), detail.

the lion, don't convey an expression, or thinking. He is always close by the lion, but as the lion begins to show his age, and the ox does not, the ox begins to seem like the big cat's silent partner, maybe caregiver or guardian. Mather calls him the lion's superego.

And although the Kingdoms eventually came to include a female lion and lion cubs, many a viewer has probably thought that the ox is female or the lion's mate—even that they are the watchful parents of the entire congregation. But imagining connections—and disconnections—between Hicks's characters, and following the changes they undergo, can absorb us for some time. Perhaps this would be the case with the work of any artist who took a fairly small, set number of figures, or characters, and continually transformed them over thirty years. There is at least one such work, I believe, and it happens to present a world that is somewhat similar to Hicks's Kingdoms.

It is George Herriman's comic strip *Krazy Kat*, which got underway around 1913 and concluded with the artist's death in 1944. On the face of it, the analogy is admittedly unexpected. Yet Herriman's creation, long acknowledged a wonderment of drawing, language, storytelling, and characterization, also revolves around animals whose feelings and demeanors are essentially human. There is Krazy Kat, a poetically innocent soul—and the strip's nominal protagonist, its lion—who is infatuated with Ignatz, a brisk, of-this-world mouse who is always looking for a chance to hurl a brick at Krazy. Ignatz is rather like the strip's leopard, its edgy and not-so-sweet second in command.

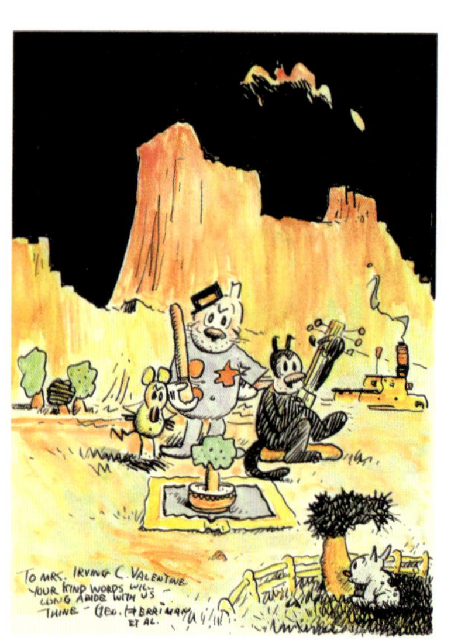

George Herriman, *Ignatz Mouse, Officer Pupp, and Krazy Kat*, c. 1925.

He and Krazy are forever under the eye of Officer Pupp, a stocky local sheriff (and dog) who is continually ready to clap Ignatz in jail for his errant behavior and who is himself smitten with Krazy. Officer Pupp, in other words, might be the strip's ox. We follow these characters over time as they plot, wax indignant, dream, dress up, and dote. Yet little ever really happens. That is part of the strip's loveliness and fascination.

Right here, however, Hicks and Herriman part ways, because as he created his Kingdoms Hicks gradually changed the situation he was presenting. His drama is of course a mute one, and we necessarily infer larger meanings from the visages of his figures and the way they are placed on their stage. From his staging, though, we come to realize that eventually Hicks had more on his mind with his characters than a statement about comity, or even their individual dispositions. They were beings he had lived with for decades, and ultimately, in pictures from his last five or six years, Hicks seems to have been as concerned with their fate, and their mortality, as he was with his own.

A Late Beginning

EXACTLY WHAT TO make of the *Peaceable Kingdoms* in the wider sphere of art and of American culture is, and is not, a settled issue. They are so familiar from reproductions, and our awareness of them is so colored by the fact that Hicks kept painting them for years, that, as much as individual ones, seen in a museum, can strike us with their beauty, their humor, and their oddness, I think we take them, as a body of pictures, for granted. We assume that one Kingdom is all a viewer needs to see. Having, on the other hand, a sense of their scope can make one excited to see as many as possible, as I have tried to suggest. But it is rare to come face to face with them in their variety.

Just as clear-cut, and as limited, is how we think about their maker. Born in 1780, as the Revolutionary War was still underway, Hicks was from, and for the nearly seven decades of his life would remain based in, Bucks County, Pennsylvania, in the northeastern part of the state, not far from Philadelphia. On wall labels next to his pictures in museums and even in many histories of American art, one generally finds little more about him than that he was a Quaker minister and a primitive or folk painter who, in making pictures of a laying down of arms, was illustrating a well-known precept of his faith and, more specifically and urgently, addressing a rift in the Society of Friends.

What is left out is that Hicks's impact as a preacher was truly wide-ranging, and that in the early nineteenth-century religion, available in any number of denominations—and the cadences of the Bible—were integral parts of many people's existences. Hicks's lifetime, as it happened, corresponded to years that saw in America, the historian Gordon S. Wood wrote, possibly the "greatest explosion of Christian religiosity since the seventeenth century or even the Reformation." The time was one, in addition, when public speaking itself, on any number of subjects, drew crowds. The lecture, wrote the literary critic F. O. Matthiessen, was the "most popular art form" of the day.

Nor do our general notions of a Quaker minister, who we might conventionally imagine to be a figure of social responsibility and unwavering good intentions, square easily with Hicks the person, who, despite his moral concerns—and his personal faith and his verbal skills—was beset with grinding anxieties. As a lengthy memoir and then a diary make clear, he struggled with a testy, highly combative, at times even violent temperament. He couldn't hold back from saying whatever was on his mind. His "unsparing tongue," his biographer wrote, became "a legend." But then he could be hit hard with remorse and a need for reconciliation.

The idea of being an artist was no less fraught. The Religious Society of Friends looked with some disapproval on the arts, and even the commercial, craftsmanly work Hicks did was grounds for concern. Being a Quaker in rural America at the time meant that, on a conscious level, one was indifferent, possibly antagonistic, to art. Like singing and dancing, art was deemed by the Society to be a wasteful, even pernicious, activity. It led away from a sought-for spiritualized life in Christ—though these thoughts were graven nowhere. There were Quakers who were highly skilled craftsmen and admired for their beautifully made utilitarian objects, and there were Quakers who were artists of a kind, most notably the Philadelphian William Bartram. But Bartram's often remarkable pictures were an aspect of his larger endeavor as a naturalist, and they were works on paper. They were not, like Hicks's paintings, good-size, substantially framed, strongly colored objects, unmissable as you walked into someone's home.

It was a pressured and murky situation, which Hicks added to by maintaining that he was certainly not a "fine" artist. His working process seemed to corroborate this. The starting points for the majority of his easel paintings, whether the Kingdoms or others, were little, black-and-white, published sources, be they prints of pictures by artists of different eras or illustrations found in Bibles, livestock manuals, gazettes, or on maps.

It is no secret that in the nineteenth century many folk artists—even professional and cosmopolitan painters on the order of Édouard Manet—employed copies of other artworks as they fashioned their pictures. The practice has been taken as a sign of strength. Holger Cahill, for instance, in an essay accompanying an exhibition of folk art at the Museum of Modern Art, wrote that these artists "borrowed freely, but borrowing has not been disdained by the greatest masters, in fact one of the signs of a vital art is the ability to assimilate the work of others."

Hicks, however, went further in that the majority of his pictures were copies in their overall schemes, and when he altered his original source image he generally added to it details taken from other publications. The results were pictures that mixed together elements taken from numerous already existing images. He may have worked this way because of prohibitions of his religion. It might have been a way of saying that the art was not his own.

Yet during the nearly thirty years that he made his easel paintings, he pushed through these religious, social, and technical constraints. His pictures were not guarded, secret artworks that only a select few could know about, nor were they meant as pleasant, anodyne souvenirs of a jolly craftsman's free moments. They were, rather, messages from him. They were often given as gifts. They may at times have been sold to raise funds for family needs—or left in the workshop as the case may be. Where they went was not the point. They were very simply works that he couldn't help but make.

Hicks brought forth his paintings from the most unusual of channels, and it shows in the way his work can be difficult to place in the rest of American art—and at the same time can be part of many disparate artistic conversations at once. Hicks shakes up our sense of American painting. His *Peaceable Kingdoms* are religious allegories, yet, accessible to viewers of any age, they have none of the solemnity or abstruseness that such a designation suggests. At the same time, they add a sense of the theatrical, the symbolical, and the strange to a national art that has such spirits in short supply. And in aspects of the Kingdoms—and of his other kinds of pictures—Hicks helpfully blurs distinctions between naive or primitive and professional painters.

By "professional," I mean mainstream, or what we generally call trained painters, though here it needs to be pointed out that these designations, like the terms naive and folk, or primitive and self-taught, are relative and often slippery. In the nineteenth century (and in earlier and later centuries), to be a professional—or a mainstream or "trained"—artist did not necessarily mean that you had taken a formal course of training in an art school. To be such an artist meant primarily that you had a conscious relation to other artistic achievements. You wanted to be part of a larger, ongoing, centuries-old conversation.

The matter has been described with great lucidity by the art historian Lorenz Eitner, writing in this case about the nineteenth-century painter Théodore Géricault. His work would seem to be the opposite of self-taught, naive, or primitive. Yet like "most of the leading painters of his century," Eitner wrote, the French Romantic "must be reckoned as an essentially self-trained artist, whose school was the museum, who chose his teachers from the masters of the past, and who, guided by instinctive sympathies, gradually defined his artistic personality by his choice of models."

It is this avid, discerning, and competitive relationship with other artists, whether of the past or one's contemporaries, that naive or folk artists tend to lack. Edward Hicks certainly did. Yet perhaps because the forms in his pictures didn't always spring out of his head but were, rather, part of a regular collaboration with various printed sources, he had more of a connection with other art than he might have realized. In his paintings of actual, historical persons and events—whether the illustrious William Penn or the signing of the Declaration of Independence—he can safely be called, striking as the pictures may be, a naive or primitive artist. Using the idiom of such a painter, however, he also created images of farm life that have a more personal and lived-in quality than folk art generally delivers. Then, in pictures whose subject is less the busy warmth of farmyards than agriculture as an ambitious enterprise, he fashioned works that, albeit naive, have a scope and breadth that many professional American painters then were bringing to the preeminent subject of the moment: the heroic landscape.

To what degree Hicks is a folk artist is a question hovering over his pictures. Any attempt to get a handle on his work means looking at him alongside these and professional artists and even with outsider artists—a designation that didn't exist in Hicks's lifetime, and wasn't on the minds of writers in the middle of the twentieth century when his qualities were first being defined. In this ambiguous spirit, one finds him, in studies of American folk art, called at different times the archetypal folk artist—perhaps primarily because he is the best known such creator—and, more accurately, the least typical of folk artists.

• • •

HICKS THE PERSON is no less unplaceable than Hicks the artist. He was a high-voltage handful. An essentially religious, passionate, and, in his words, "uncommonly dogmatical disputant," he was insistent on his own brand of belief and intolerant of, even abusive toward, those who didn't toe his idea of the line. In the Quaker community, he saw those Friends who espoused ideas that were different from his as enemies of the truth.

Yet Hicks could realize at times that he wasn't very different from people he disagreed with. Especially as a young adult, his contrition over his vituperativeness—or his near "despair" one day when his words were questioned by a group of elders and he hotly defended himself—could leave him flattened. After one such occasion, he wrote that "had I been of a melancholy complexion I might have been tempted to commit suicide." He was prone to seeing himself as guilty of one thing or another and he confessed more than once that he felt he had achieved nothing of significance. Running alongside all of this was his humor. He had, as he wrote, "a natural fund of nonsense." He was, Eleanore Price Mather saw, "a born entertainer" (in some sense his easel paintings and his preaching could both be viewed as entertainments). And, although one does not necessarily follow from the other, he invariably became impatient with people he thought were indulging states of despondency.

He couldn't, however, help feeling bad about his levity and liveliness. It was another thing to keep him on edge, or, to use a word he often had at hand, "straitened." "Seriously thoughtful about talking too much," he wrote in a characteristic moment. He saw himself, as he put it, possessed by a "zig-zag nature" which "predisposes me to extremes"—and sometimes the pull in his emotions must have leveled him. "Oh!," he notes at one point, brooding about his silence at recent meetings and unguarded chattering at other times, "that I may be preserved from being a dead, formal preacher, and light, idle jester." There could be tension wherever he turned, even when describing the day before him: "I am not well enough to work, and I am not sick enough to be confined to my house or bed."

The whiplash so evident in Hicks's vehement and never hidden emotions—qualities one wants to call Dostoevskian—may have derived from his biography. It is a story of, in its most elemental form, having something, losing it, then replacing it with something else. Hicks came from a long-settled and mostly New England–based family of distinguished professional attainment, often in law and civil service. But during the Revolution his paternal grandfather's Tory sympathies wound up stripping the family of its wealth. Impoverishment, along with the death of his mother when he was not yet two, forced his father to have Edward brought up in a foster home. The Twinings, his adoptive parents, were Quakers, and by his early twenties Edward—at the time a rowdy, a drinker, a singer all the journey long, and a flirter with girls—converted to Quakerism.

The proper Quaker term, however, is not converted. It is convinced. He became a convinced Friend. The very word is in keeping with the progressive, enlightened, and egalitarian tenor of the Society of Friends. The highly democratic nature of the faith—seen, for example, in the parity women had with men in many positions of authority—gave Edward a way of looking at, or to be more precise, a way of judging, the wealth, privilege, and learning that he just missed having.

As a thirteen-year-old, he became indentured to local coach makers. In the seven years under their tutelage, he learned carriage repair and the painting of carriages, which he clearly gravitated toward. By his early twenties, Hicks had set up his own shop for such work. Commercial painting of one sort or another was how, for the rest of his life, he supported himself, his wife Sarah—known as Sally—and their four daughters and one son.

There was a short time, though, when this wasn't the case. In 1814, in his mid-thirties and now a minister and father, Hicks decided to give up the skills he had learned and become a farmer. Motivated perhaps by mixed feelings over being a Quaker minister who did commercial paint jobs—and sensing as well that farming better fulfilled his belief in the spiritual superiority of "humble industry"—he bought eighteen acres to farm, in Newtown. Helped principally by his young son Isaac, he grew wheat, corn, and oats and raised pigs and turkeys, selling to neighbors whatever the family didn't need. But he had little aptitude for the venture, and soon he returned to the work he knew.

As a commercial painter, he took orders for decorating, or, in effect, finishing, a range of vehicles, including gigs, sulkies, coaches, wagons, and sleighs. When the orders weren't local, he could hand deliver the product, even traveling out of state to do so. In his shop, which had the services of a stream of young assistants over the years, he painted street directionals and signs for local taverns and tradesmen, and he was available for ornamenting clock faces, boxes, chairs, desks, inkstands, and other objects. House painting jobs were eventually handled by his assistants. Most of his decorative work and his signs have, unfortunately, been lost. Among his shop hands were a relative, Thomas Hicks, Edward's first cousin once removed, who became a nationally-known portraitist in his day, and Martin Johnson Heade, who became one of the odder, livelier, and least predictable figures in American art of any era—and, in one aspect of his work, very possibly Edward's heir.

• • •

LIKE A NUMBER of other self-taught artists, Hicks was a late beginner when it came to making his own art. He seems to have fashioned his first independent, or easel, painting, which was a *Peaceable Kingdom*, around 1818 or so, when he was in his late thirties (though the first Kingdom that can be definitively dated is from 1826). It is thought that, over the next three decades, he created about two Kingdoms a year. They are without question his signal contribution to art; and while with some he is merely repeating himself, and with others he is clearly inspired, it is as a single endeavor that they have the most meaning.

His pictures on historical and national themes aren't the works of originality that the Kingdoms are, but in some instances, they are lovely and even striking. George Washington just before he crossed the Delaware River was a favorite topic, in part because the general's famous surprise attack on the British was a source of pride for a Bucks County native and was especially alive for someone like Hicks, because Washington was based at the time in Newtown. Hicks's feeling for Washington transcended his regional connection, however. Along with many Americans of the early nineteenth century—particularly those who grew up in the 1780s and 1790s, the years right after the war for independence had been won—Hicks carried with him a proprietary and somewhat hallowed idea of the American Revolution. In this reverential light, he took the signing of the Declaration of Independence as a subject on a number of occasions. In his library there was a much-consulted book on the lives of the signers.

The finest of these works on overtly American themes may be his two quite similar versions of *The Falls of Niagara*. Hicks's image, in which we see a badger, a snake, a moose, and an eagle in the foreground, and the Falls are small and relegated to the distance, was taken from a drawing on a map. In spirit, the image is a cousin of the *Peaceable Kingdoms*. It is a gathering of creatures, set to the side of the scene, though not, as with the Kingdoms, fully dominating it. By the time he created the works, which are painted in a mellifluous array of earth and wood colors, Hicks had made the challenging trip to the Falls. He was inspired to go after reading *The Foresters*, Alexander Wilson's small, book-length poem about his own journey, undertaken in the fall of 1804, to Niagara.

One can see how this still quite readable and at times really lovely narrative might have called out to Hicks. (In thanks, he incorporated lines from the poem onto the frames of these pictures.) Wilson, who was based in Philadelphia—he would later become the country's first important ornithologist—set out with his two companion foresters on a route taking them

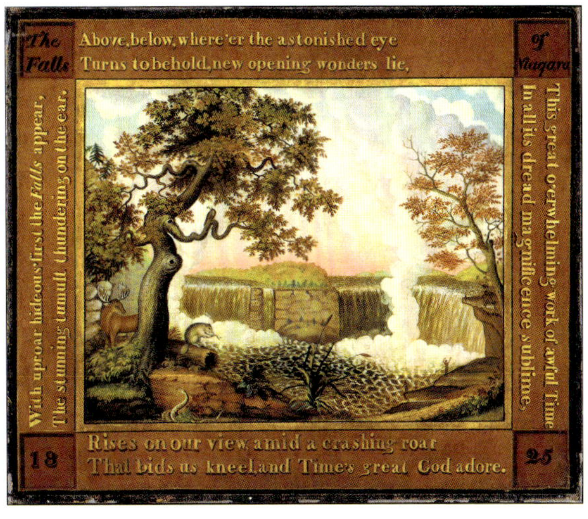

Edward Hicks, *The Falls of Niagara*, c. 1825, 31 ½ × 38 in. (80 × 96.5 cm).

Through fertile Bucks, where lofty barns abound
For wheat, fair Quakers, eggs, and fruit renowned

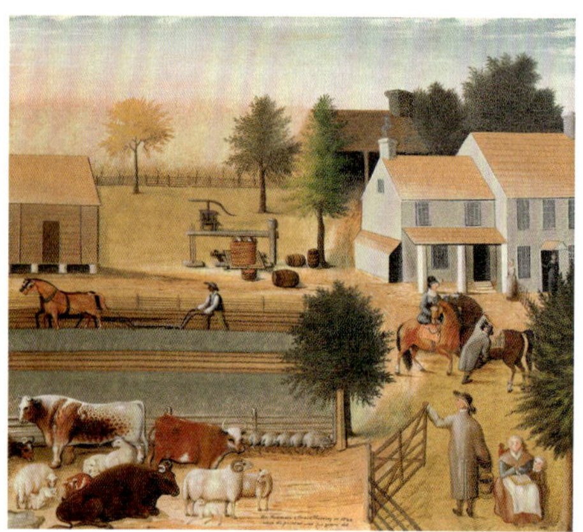

Edward Hicks, *The Residence of David Twining*, c. 1845–46, 26 × 29 ½ in. (66 × 74.9 cm).

Along the way the bard, as Wilson playfully refers to himself, describes, in addition to the people they encounter and the birds they see, the threats that settlers faced nightly from bears, wolves, and what people called panthers (he identifies them as a kind of cougar). Reading *The Foresters*, we see how little different much of America in the early decades of the nineteenth century was from the world of Isaiah's verses.

But then midway through the 1840s, when he was in his mid-sixties, a change came over Hicks. He began to work with greater freedom and industry. He started making the most distinctively different kinds of Kingdoms and, too, his paintings of Bucks County farms. The farm pictures and another late work, *Noah's Ark*, have been much admired by commentators on Hicks. *Noah's Ark* has been called by many one of the most beautiful paintings he made. But like the farm scenes, it has somehow not been worked into a wider sense of the creator of the Kingdoms, let alone into the bloodstream of American painting in general. At the Philadelphia Museum of Art, which owns *Noah's Ark*, the picture, when hanging, is generally found in a section containing rustic or country period furniture and artifacts, meaning that the work, like the artist, is a little hidden.

In his last years, Hicks had entered a new terrain as an artist. He was doing pictures that, although small in number, put in a different light the work he had done before. This is an unusual development among nineteenth-century American painters, and it almost exclusively occurs with artists we see as trained, or part of the mainstream. One finds it happening with Fitz Henry Lane, whose late marines and coastal scenes strike a forlorn, end-of-season note that until then had not been part of his art, and with Winslow Homer, who in his last years, at least in his oil paintings, largely gave up making pictures of people and withdrew, as his canvases show, into a rugged communion with pounding waves and rocky shorelines.

The late work of both New England artists has about it a facing up to elemental realizations. Hicks's pictures from the latter half of the 1840s, however, are expansive. He seems to be lifting the curtains on his stage. He appears to be realizing promises that had been there in him all along.

• • •

I HAVE SAID that Edward Hicks is somehow invisible for us. This is not to say that his pictures, life, and thinking have gone unexamined. Hicks has been described with real sensitivity—but by writers who have looked at him primarily as a Quaker and studied his pictures in light of this connection. In Alice Ford's richly detailed 1952 biography, in Carolyn Weekley's scrupulous 1999 marshalling of seemingly everything known about Hicks, and in the highly sensitive, speculative writing from different times by Eleanore Price Mather—and in a single, penetrating essay from 1981 by David Tatham—a breathing whole has been made out of Hicks's different kinds of pictures and the raft of documentary information concerning his person, his family, and his religious milieu. In the writings of Edna S. Pullinger, we are given, lastly, a close-up view of aspects of the Hicks who spent most of his life in the small universe of Newtown, PA.

But what his relation might be to other nineteenth-century American painters—of any stripe—is rarely encountered. David Tatham, whose voice is an isolated one in American art writing, at least suggested that Hicks might well be seen on the larger stage of American Romanticism. He saw that there might be similarities between the Pennsylvania artist and, say, Thomas Cole, the founder of the idea of an American landscape school. Hicks was certainly of his time in making Niagara Falls a theme.

Artists of every variety in the decades before the Civil War wanted to put their stamp on this resplendent natural wonder, and it brought out superlative examples in a range of approaches. John Trumbull, whose best-known pictures are (dreary and overbearing) scenes of moments from the Revolution, showed that he could be a painter of real elegance in two paintings of the Falls that suavely contrast the bright white of the gushing water against a surrounding darkness. Trumbull's paintings are in the Wadsworth Atheneum, whose collection includes some of the liveliest of all pictures of the Falls. John F. Kensett, who possessed the subtlest mind—and painter's hand—among American landscapists of the nineteenth century, is represented in the Hartford museum with a powerful and unexpected take on the subject: a close-up of huge red rocks, with the pounding water forming a white backdrop. This is one of the most adventurous and unexpected compositions in his work. Niagara's rising vapor almost takes over another masterpiece in the Atheneum, a work by Thomas Chambers that scintillatingly plays off the scalloped edges of the cottony puffs of the vapor with the dark, scalloped-edged forms of trees and rocks.

It is not surprising that the Falls was the subject of one of the most famous American paintings of the nineteenth century: Frederic Church's unorthodox, amazingly detailed, lateral view of Horseshoe Falls—an enormous canvas that, shown on its own, drew crowds in London as well as New York. More phenomenal, I think, is a small gouache by George Catlin, who came up with a bird's-eye view of the Falls and the entire surrounding area. It could, on a quick first view, be taken as an abstraction. It explains what even visitors to the area can find hard to understand, which is how the Falls are part of the surrounding space.

Hicks's two similar paintings of the subject easily hold their own with these distinctive works, and not only because their tawny colors, with the yellow-gold lettering on their frames (from Wilson's poem), are warmly beautiful in themselves. Hicks stands out among his contemporaries in that landscape in itself was not enough for him. He needed to populate any terrain with sentient beings, and his snake, who, amusingly, seems to appraise us in both versions of the Niagara scenes, gives the paintings an inner consciousness we can identify with.

But Hicks's connection to the larger themes of his time went beyond his feeling for the Falls. His *Peaceable Kingdom*s might without exaggeration be seen as kin to other large-spirited and ongoing undertakings in the visual arts during the prewar years. I have in mind Alexander Wilson's nine-volume *American Ornithology,* George Catlin's portraits of Native Americans and his views of the West, and John James Audubon's *Birds of America*. The time was one of a heightened national self-

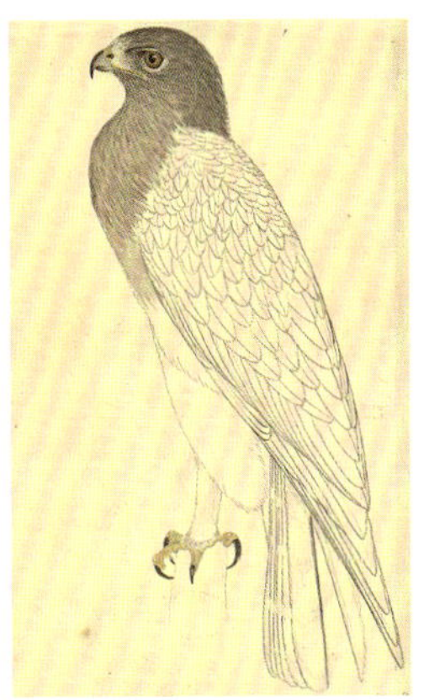

Alexander Wilson, *Rough-legged Hawk.*

awareness. It was a moment for projects that could convey the sense of abundance that Americans felt marked their country. It was also, of course, when American writing, found in essays, stories, novels, and poems by some half-dozen authors whom we continue to read, came into its own.

As Irving Howe wrote in *The American Newness*, his acute 1986 study of Ralph Waldo Emerson—and the strain of Emersonian confidence running through American thinking—there was an increasing certitude in the 1830s and 1840s that the United States had made good on its Revolution. The country had become a rare instance in world history: it was proving itself a supple, self-assured, functioning democratic republic. And this example was being set, as writers and painters of the time, and their audiences, were certain, in a natural paradise of sorts.

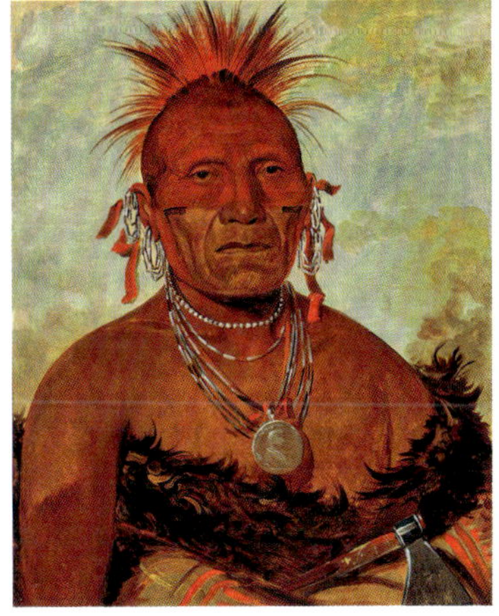

George Catlin, *Shón-ka-ki-he-ga, Horse Chief, Grand Pawnee Head Chief,* 1832, 29 × 24 in. (73.7 × 60.9 cm).

Historians, particularly in recent years, have shown the period in a less heroic and more modulated light. Social inequalities, racism, and financial upheavals were hardly unknown (as Howe well understood) in the yeoman's paradise. With cotton production being stepped up, slavery—the cancer in this Eden—was becoming even more entrenched. Andrew Jackson, the president who embodied the new mass energies, and was the first American national leader who did not come from or represent the settled, almost elitist values of Virginia or Massachusetts, was ruthless in his leveling of the lives of Native Americans. (He was the subject of a hasty portrait by Hicks, who was by and large not a Jackson man.) Yet as Richard Chase put it in 1955, in his *Walt Whitman Reconsidered*—in words that still, a little shakily, call out to us—"It is possible, in moods of pessimism and nostalgia, to think that the years between 1820 and 1860 were the best this country is destined to know."

Hicks was certainly aware of the larger, moral "newness" of his country. His writing indicates that he understood that the United States was an experiment in democratic governing that the world had not known before, and it isn't farfetched to see the Kingdoms as visual metaphors of this tenuous experiment. The pictures are, after all, about diversities held in suspension for a larger, common purpose. In some paintings he included in his assembly Hebe, the goddess of youth, and he gave her the American eagle as a companion.

Yet it could also be said that Hicks touched something deeper in the national psyche than Catlin or Cole (or many other artists) did in that his Kingdoms appear to have grown out of, and to have been a comment on, incompatibilities among one people. His already mentioned impetus (or partial impetus) was strife in the Society of Friends. It was a dispute between Quakers living in cities who had come to want the Society to be more like traditional religions, with set, outward displays of piety, and Quakers, like Edward, who lived in the country, were generally not as materially comfortable as their urban brethren, and wished Quakerism to hold true to its mystical original spirit—to its belief that formalized religious observance could only hinder a person from coming to a deeper awareness of life.

The dispute was more than theological. It was about what it meant to be Quaker, and it is fascinating to think of Hicks returning again and again to the image of what might be called factionalism resolved because it mirrors the tense debate the country as a whole was having. In the 1840s and 1850s, as American life was overtaken with questions of how to contain or extend slavery, the subject of hostilities within one family became the sometimes literal bloody national story, and these hostilities became actual war in 1861. Whether one sees the Kingdoms as picturing a sweet accord or an uncertain truce, they are about inherent, inescapable polarities. They may be among the only American artworks of their or any time with this theme. As such—and if we wanted to see the paintings as being principally about the national character—they could even be comments on the divisiveness that in recent years has choked American life.

• • •

IT TAKES AN EFFORT, of course, to see paintings by self-taught or primitive artists installed in a museum alongside those by artists versed in the conventions of a naturalistic way of representing reality. Our eyes and minds have not been conditioned to do this, and simply to blend the two kinds of work (which rarely happens) can be as dissatisfying as the long-standing practice of keeping them firmly separated. Much depends on the actual works at hand and the sensitivity with which they are juxtaposed. Because of his renown, museums tend at least to keep the Hicks work (or works) in their collections on view somewhere, though it often seems that not a lot of thought has been given to the matter.

Were the Kingdoms to be displayed outside the precincts of naive art, one reasonable place might be along with all sorts of intimately-sized pictures of people. We almost cannot help seeing Hicks's animals as human beings of a sort, and there are instances where pictures by him come close to works by professional, mainstream artists.

It is often enlivening, for example, when painters of people show a character in a scene making direct eye contact with the viewer. It can make a picture seem as if it has broken through the conventions of a particular long gone era. Unlike most naive painters, and unlike most run-of-the-mill professional painters of genre scenes, Hicks does this. The leopard and the young lion occasionally look out at the viewing audience, and it is always fun to imagine that the leopard is wondering about us. And while it may be merely coincidental, a figure (or possibly two) glances pointedly at us in a number of pictures by contemporaries and near-contemporaries of Hicks whose art is much more than run-of-the-mill.

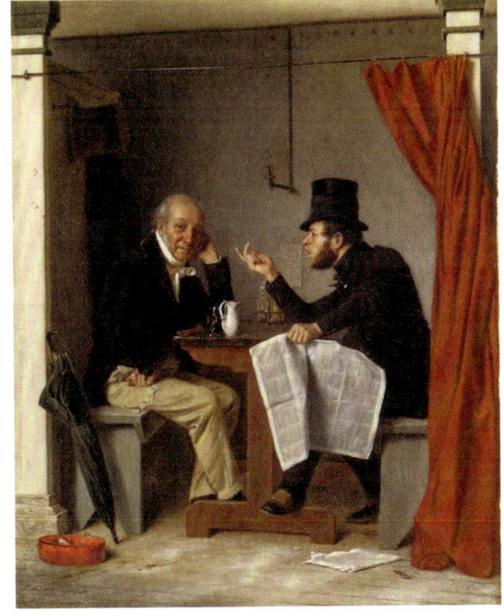

Richard Caton Woodville, *Politics in an Oyster House*, 1848, 16 1/4 × 13 1/16 in. (41.2 × 33.1 cm).

Actually, we encounter it in a number of masterpieces of nineteenth-century American painting. It is spooky when, in Thomas Eakins's 1874 *Starting Out after Rail*, one of the hunters in the boat

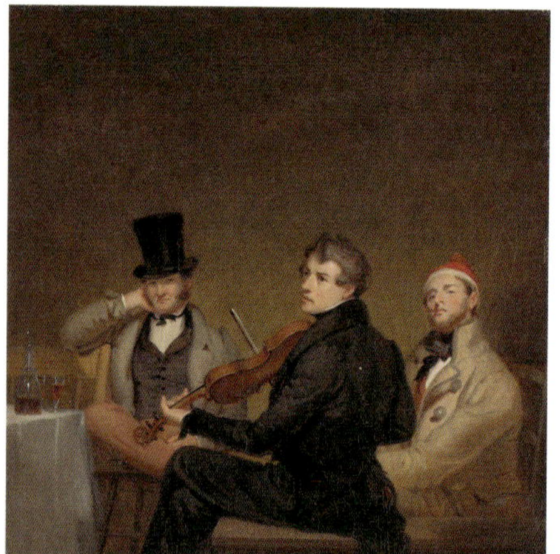

William Sidney Mount, *After Dinner*, 1834, 10 7/8 × 10 15/16 in. (27.6 × 27.8 cm).

casually turns to catch our attention; and we are stared at by figures in George Caleb Bingham's strongest river scenes, including his 1846 *Boatmen on the Missouri*. In Richard Caton Woodville's *Politics in an Oyster House*, the older man looks at us, as the young newspaper-grasping man makes his points, with an expression that could mean "Can you believe this fella?"—though part of the beauty of the picture is that we don't know at all what he is thinking. And in William Sidney Mount's *After Dinner*, one of the artist's rare works where his figures are entirely convincing—where their expressions are not coated in a stagy good nature—the listeners of the musician wander with their eyes in our direction.

When, especially in a few Kingdoms from the 1830s, the lion looks directly at the viewer, the emotion is different from when the leopard does it. The lion confronts us in a raw and fierce way. His eyes tell us he is in a state of turmoil—and that state hardly exists in the work of any of Hicks's contemporaries, no matter what their technical capacities. It is as if we are looking at a nascent American Expressionism.

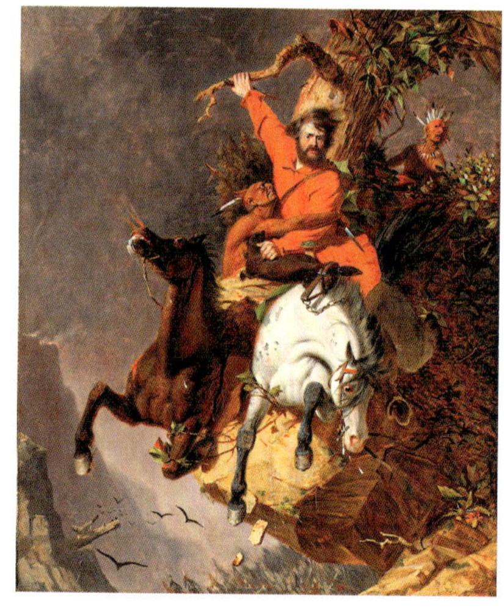

Charles Deas, *The Death Struggle*, 1840–45, 30 × 25 in. (76.2 × 63.5 cm).

By comparison the distress and violence in an often reproduced 1845 painting by Charles Deas entitled *The Death Struggle*, which shows a white backwoodsman gripped by a Native American and both plunging on their horses to certain death, suggests a scene out of an adventure book for boys. (If there is an edge of the genuinely nightmarish about

The Death Struggle, it may have something to do with the fact that Deas, who was a finely skilled and sometimes exquisite painter, particularly of trappers and Native Americans, lost his mental bearings a few years after making the picture. Barely thirty years old at the time, he would spend the rest of his life in asylums in and around New York City.)

Yet the strained and hallucinatory atmosphere of some Kingdoms, or the melancholy and autumnal mood of others—or the mood conveyed by the knowing look of the leopard in some pictures, occasionally recalling to me the look that the nude young woman in Manet's *Olympia* casts in our direction—aren't states that we are geared to take altogether seriously. We set them aside as childlike or outlandish. This shortchanges Hicks and American painting.

• • •

FOR THE MAJORITY OF VIEWERS, Hicks is simply, uncomplicatedly synonymous with folk art. As it happened, his lifetime corresponded to the years, from right after the Revolution to the 1840s or so, when folk art creations showed their greatest vitality, delicacy, and unexpectedness. His rediscovery in the early 1930s, furthermore, precisely coincided with the beginning of the widespread appreciation of this kind of work. Prior to this time oil paintings by self-taught artists—and the metal weathervanes, duck decoys, whirligigs, birth and death certificates ornamented in watercolor, tinware, scrimshaw, samplers, farm tools, ship figureheads, cigar store Indians, carved wood toys, cookie molds, and other items made by craftspersons, schoolchildren, sailors, and anyone else with the needed spare time—had been the concern chiefly of local antiquarian societies. It was in a fair of antiques and local crafts in Bucks County, in 1882, that a few of Hicks's pictures first surfaced after his death. (Then they returned to oblivion for another half century.)

After the First World War, however, artists began to look at these unassuming and sometimes crude, but also often ingenious and deft, artifacts with curiosity and excitement, frequently first encountering the pieces in antiques stores near where they went for summer vacations. Painters and sculptors, and later curators and collectors, saw in the flatness of the forms and the bright, unmodulated colors of the pictures—and in the boldness and brusqueness of outline of the carved and assembled toys and weathervanes—a sense of daring, insouciance, and freedom that were remarkably in tune with the way the most powerful European artists had been thinking for years. It has been said with much truth—and elaborated on by Elizabeth Stillinger in *A Kind of Archeology: Collecting American Folk Art, 1876–1976*—that an appreciation of nineteenth-century American primitive art and artifacts was a collateral gift of the revolution in art that began with the Impressionists and Post-Impressionists.

Soon, this work, now increasingly called folk art, newly became the subject of museum exhibitions. The effort was spearheaded by Holger Cahill, a journalist who aimed to write fiction but who had a gift for arts administration and creating publicity. Cahill was drawn to objects that were artistically alive, but he was less concerned with the distinctive talent of the individual folk creator. He saw folk art as being about impersonal and age-old craft traditions. Working as a publicist at the Newark Museum in the 1920s led to his organizing exhibitions of folk art painting there in 1930 and folk art sculpture the following year. These fledgling endeavors were capped by his exhibition in 1932, entitled *American Folk Art*, at the Museum of Modern Art (itself a fledgling, having been created in 1929). The show's subtitle, *The Art of the Common Man in America, 1750–1900*, made clear Cahill's larger point in the matter.

Weathervanes, portraits, mourning pictures on velvet, and the occasional *Peaceable Kingdom*, among other items, could soon be seen in elegantly laid out selling shows in galleries. This was certainly the case with Edith Gregor Halpert's Downtown Gallery, on West 13th Street in New York City. By 1931, Cahill had convinced Halpert, who handled contemporary artists such as Stuart Davis and Yasuo Kuniyoshi, of the commercial and aesthetic significance of folk art. That year they became partners in the American Folk Art Gallery, which was given its own floor in Halpert's townhouse space. It became a fixture of the Downtown Gallery (even when it moved uptown) and was long the most remunerative part of Halpert's enterprise.

The days when paintings or carvings by untrained artists, chalkware figurines, or decorated furniture were items you would find half-buried in rural attics or jumbled together in dusty antiques stores on Second

Avenue were beginning to be over. Writers now started in on systematic studies of the material; and while people had collected it before—most notably the sculptor Elie Nadelman and his wife Viola, who opened a folk art museum in Riverdale, in the northern reaches of New York City, in 1926—searching it out now was a less rarefied endeavor.

Among these more recent appreciators was Abby Aldrich Rockefeller, who, much aided by the expertise and the finds of Cahill and Halpert, was attracted to the work of self-taught artists and craftspersons primarily for its affinities, in formal ways, with modern art. (This was less the case with the Nadelmans, whose collection had a more encyclopedic and ethnographic tone to it.) Mrs. Rockefeller's initial holdings of American primitive art—a substantial group was put together almost overnight by Cahill and Halpert—became the basis of Cahill's 1932 show at the Modern. Many of the pieces, including a Hicks painting dated 1846–47 of the Twining residence, went, at least at first, into the museum's collection. In her New York City home on West 54th Street, Mrs. Rockefeller interspersed her American primitive pictures with her collection of modern painters.

At least one modern painter was particularly struck by Hicks. When, in 1931, Fernand Léger laid eyes on a *Peaceable Kingdom* in New York, he called it the "greatest painting" he had seen in the country. He remarked that as far as he was concerned Hicks was a "more important" figure than Henri Rousseau, the doyen of untaught painters. Might Léger have believed this because Hicks, as a manipulator of his materials, is often a more assertive and vibrant painter than Rousseau? Léger's views, arriving at the moment when a new realm of art was being unearthed, proved worthy of a small article in *The Art Digest*.

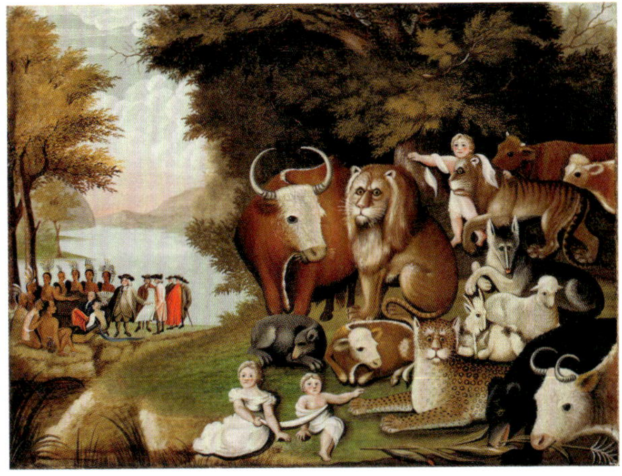

Edward Hicks, *Peaceable Kingdom*, c. 1833, 17 1⁄2 × 23 11⁄16 in. (44.5 × 60.2 cm).

From practically the moment they began to be seen in the early 1930s, *Peaceable Kingdoms* became, as it were, one of the representative faces of American folk art. A brilliant example (on page 37) was purchased by a public collection—the Worcester Art Museum—already in 1934. The very words "peaceable kingdom," which are not in Isaiah and probably appeared first in the illustration Hicks used as his starting point, were helpful in this regard. They suggested the innocuousness that clings to the idea of the folk spirit. The artist's name itself loosely connected him to it. As a noun or adjective, "hick" means, of course, provincial and unsophisticated, though the reality is different. The family surname Hicks dates to the 1300s (if not earlier) and is associated with many illustrious and not especially provincial figures on a number of continents.

Elizabeth Stillinger convincingly writes that Cahill, Halpert, and Mrs. Rockefeller were the "triumvirate that put folk art on the road to acceptance as art rather than as history or ethnology, and that stimulated its popular acceptance." But others were especially focused on Hicks. In searches that began in the 1930s, the Philadelphia art dealer Robert Carlen would eventually locate and purchase more than thirty pictures by him. Believing virtually on first sight that Hicks was a "great artist," Carlen was closer to being a fan of the Quaker painter and less concerned than Halpert with placing the paintings in important collections. Carlen's 1949 Hicks exhibition, marking the centennial of the artist's death, was one of the earliest one-person shows Hicks had.

The exhibition came at the moment when the writer Alice Ford was in the midst of research that would result in her biography of the artist. Ford was aware of Carlen's own research, as letters to him make clear. For many years he operated as an art historian, antiquarian, and detective combined, ready to travel anywhere in his station wagon to turn up buried pictures. Ford told Carlen that there was a "widespread" impression in Bucks County that he was also writing a biography, and she had heard that a dealer in Trenton named Leonardo L. Beans might be writing on Hicks, too. At the same time, Jean Lipman, an authority on folk art and the editor of *Art in America*, was planning an all-Hicks issue for 1950; and Dorothy Miller, who was married to Holger Cahill and becoming one of the foremost curators at the Museum of Modern Art, was then embarked on a catalogue of Hicks's paintings.

In the midst of all of this activity around the artist, Ford wanted Carlen (and undoubtedly everyone else) to know that she had sole access to any family papers and that her findings would "astonish" anyone interested in the subject. Her *Edward Hicks: Painter of the Peaceable Kingdom,* published in 1952, sustained her claim. It was an achievement in research that was probably equal to anything that had been done by then on Eakins or Homer and certainly went further than scholarship on Albert Pinkham Ryder. At the time, to give the situation a little more perspective, people were only beginning to become acquainted with artists of the caliber of Raphaelle Peale, Martin Johnson Heade, and John F. Peto; and while the subject of nineteenth-century American landscape painting was hardly virgin terrain, most of the landscapists were only hazily known. When *The Landscapes of Frederic Edwin Church* appeared in 1966, its author, David Huntington, could write with the excitement of someone revealing a long lost colossus.

The interest in Hicks and folk art in general was such that it generated backlashes. Two of the best writers attracted to the subject of older American art, E. P. Richardson and James Thomas Flexner, both felt that this kind of work was being overrated, though they realized, without saying much about him, that Hicks stood apart as a figure of undeniable force and conviction. The art historian Julius Held, in a scholarly article published in 1951, went further in trying to quell the enthusiasm (and he brought into his article the opinions of Virgil Barker, another art historian who was similarly dubious).

Bothered by the claims made for the Quaker painter that, as a naïf or an innocent, he was a kind of "noble savage" whose works sprang from nowhere, Held, whose primary concerns were Rubens and Rembrandt, painstakingly tried to link Hicks's Kingdoms to age-old artistic traditions. In showing, however, that there are pictures and sculptures of different varieties and eras that touch on the idea of a pacified assembly of beasts—whether showing Adam naming the animals or Orpheus playing his lyre—Held inadvertently gave Hicks's theme an added depth and stature. The art historian also helpfully answered a question that some viewers eventually arrive at: Did artists do versions of Isaiah's prophesy before Hicks? One of the "very rare illustrations" of it, Held revealed, can be found on a relief at the Duomo in Orvieto.

• • •

In the self-contained world of folk art appreciation today, Hicks has passed into being, it would seem, a kind of eminent old chestnut. In the exhibition of Barbara Gordon's collection devoted to the subject, *A Shared Legacy: Folk Art in America* (which is traveling as I write), a detail of a *Peaceable Kingdom* forms the catalogue's cover, and in Gordon's preface, she writes, in effect, that obtaining this Hicks completed her endeavor. Talking about how her children had to put up over the years with her activity as a collector, she says, "When I finally was able to purchase *The Peaceable Kingdom* by Edward Hicks, a lifelong dream, I went on a walk with Caroline to tell her the good news. Before I got the words out, she said 'Don't tell me, you got *The Peaceable Kingdom*!'"

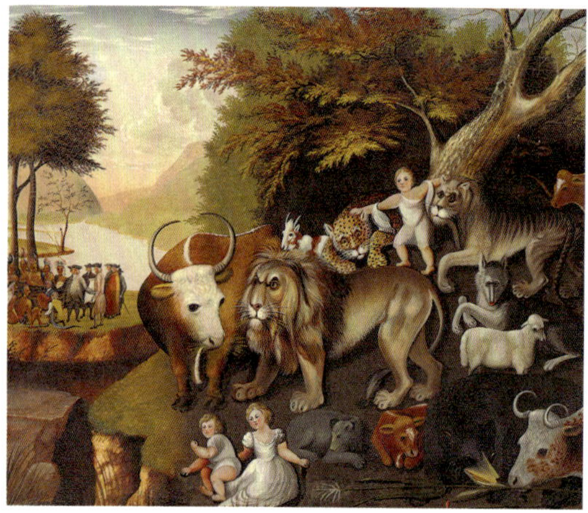

Edward Hicks, *Peaceable Kingdom*, 1835–40, 26 × 29 1⁄2 in. (66 × 74.9 cm).

Gordon's collection is a very fine and traditional one. In addition to its mighty Kingdom—the lion is one of Hicks's most fiercely patriarchal—it includes a striking painting from around 1854 by John Hilling of the burning (by arsonists) of the Old South Church in Bath, Maine. There are also distinctive works by better-known folk painters of the time, James Bard and Jurgan Frederick Huge (pronounced u-gay), both of whom painted boats—though Huge, who when not painting was a grocer in Bridgeport, Connecticut, is at his most extraordinary in two panoramically wide and amazingly detailed fantasy townscapes (that are not part of the Gordon collection).

Most of *A Shared Legacy*, however, is not Hicks or Bard, Huge or Hilling. Along with portraits by Ammi Phillips and others, it is comprised of cigar-store figures, painted chests, carousel figures, trade signs—a painted white set of teeth, used for a dentist's office—decoys, wood and chalkware figurines, whirligigs, decorated boxes, dressing tables, and pages from ornamented family record books. These many works all somehow cohere, not only because they were mostly made for consumers in rural America in the antebellum era but because, since the show that Cahill mounted at the Modern in 1932, these kinds of pictures and objects have always been seen together. *A Shared Legacy* is one in a long string of exhibitions (and books) of a similar makeup.

Yet having a whirligig on the back cover of this show's catalogue, to match the Kingdom on the front, and seeing Hicks in the company of these objects—even considering that as a commercial painter he decorated furniture and clock faces himself—is to keep him stuck in all too peaceable a kingdom. The time has come not only to imagine his work alongside that of established nineteenth-century American painters but in the company of creators who are closer to us in spirit. These are outsider artists, or figures who operate outside the main developments of art.

Outsider art has never been a movement and the word itself is subject to question. For some commentators, the designation "self-taught" is a more neutral and objective term, and recently the word "outlier" has been proposed; I will use "outsider" because, having been in continuous use now for half a century, it focuses the mind more quickly and sharply than other terms. Whatever it is called, this diverse work, which has been made by men and women in different countries, primarily in the twentieth century, takes as many forms as there are outsider artists. Initially, the term was associated with people who made art despite, or perhaps because of, their states of mental or physical impairment—people such as the Swiss Adolf Wölfli, who created fantastically intricate game board–like images, or the Mexican-American Martín Ramírez, who fashioned, with a reliance on parallel lines, a rhythmic realm of tunnels, trains, and mountains.

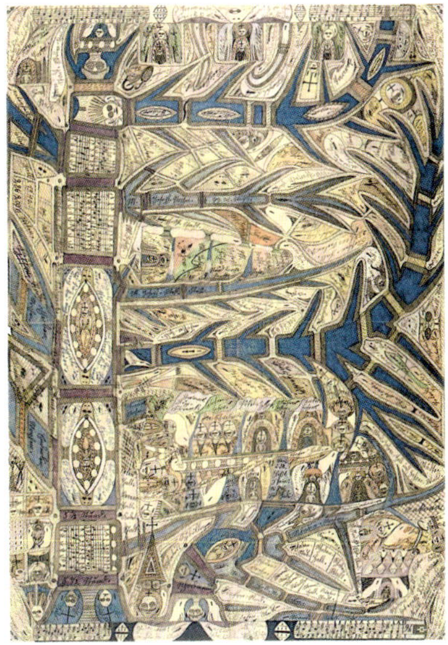

Adolf Wölfli, *Rhodanus, Spain*, 1910, 39 1/4 × 28 1/4 in. (99.7 × 71.7 cm).

Wölfli and Ramírez first began making art after mental breakdowns brought about lifelong confinement in psychiatric hospitals. In

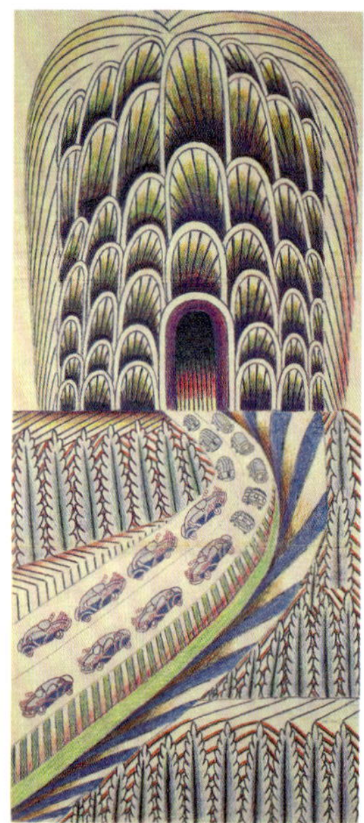

Martín Ramírez, *Untitled*, 1954, 52 3/16 × 23 15/16 in. (132.6 × 60.8 cm).

their elaborate and often large drawings, or in the equally imposing works on paper by Henry Darger, who lived as a recluse in Chicago and whose pictures often show squads of young girls fending off attackers, a viewer is given, it seems, maps of beguiling but also at times nightmarish terrains. We see images that can recall the irrational imaginings of the Surrealists but also have a singlemindedness, a sense of a vision pursued without deviation, that is different from Surrealism.

In recent decades outsider art has also come to be connected very often (but not exclusively) with the creations of people who were black and lived restricted existences in the segregated South. They were not mentally unbalanced or institutionalized but made their paintings or carvings—or quilts, metal sculptures, or constructions in wire or foil—out of their respective personal desires and needs, with little or no thought of established art forms. In this second wave, as it were, of outsiderdom, many of the most alluring works were created with a seeming improvisatory, almost rash, freedom, whether the abstract wall hangings of Mary Lee Bendolph (of Gee's Bend renown) or Rosie Lee Tompkins, or the rough-hewn paintings of animals and city sites by William Hawkins, who often added, at the bottom of his pictures, along with his prominently large name, his birth date. The spirit and the stories of the Bible, done with an appealing naiveté, form the subject of another seemingly speedy creator, the New Orleans street preacher Sister Gertrude Morgan.

Outsider art and folk art are not entirely different from each other, and, eerily, they came into the spotlight in eras when mainstream art was, one might say, practically waiting for their respective alternative spirits. Becoming known in the middle decades of the twentieth century, folk art had an eye-opening appeal because, like the professional and progressive art of the time, it seemed to be about the power of shape and form. It showed how much art could do without naturalistically conceived and academically polished figures, tones of color, and space. Outsider art, in turn, which has been exhibited and analyzed with increasing care in the last number of decades, has found a ready audience because, in this time, many professional and progressive artists have sought to create bodies of work that mirror their own, particular thinking. For a long while, we have been living in a kind of outsider moment: a period when larger movements or styles—styles which are widely presumed to embody some aesthetic progress or progression—hardly exist. It is a moment when each artist forms a school of one.

Although we don't think of outsider art in relation to the nineteenth century, a number of highly idiosyncratic figures from that time—William Blake, and to a greater extent Victor Hugo in his drawings—might be called outsiders, and so might Edward Hicks. To see him in this light helps clarify, in any event, ways in which "folk artist" is not the entirely right way to describe him. He wasn't an outsider if the term is used to suggest that he was an isolate or physically or mentally impaired. Like some of the figures in the second wave of artists to be called outsiders, he was, on the contrary, very much a visible and active member of his community. He knew a great number of people in his capacity as minister and as a craftsman, whether he was repairing carriages, painting houses, or decorating and fixing furniture of all varieties. He was enough of a businessman to buy for his apprentices the clothes he wanted them to work in.

The signs he painted, be they for a tavern, a library, a bridge, or as street markers, "could be seen," Edna S. Pullinger writes, "all over Newtown." Friends and customers would drop by his paint shop, which was over his carriage house, itself connected to the house the Hicks family lived in. The handsome stone dwelling, on what is now Penn Street, which he built in 1821 and lived in for the rest of his life, could hardly have been more centrally situated. From the back, it was a little walk across the grass to the Newtown Meeting. Over the years a home or two have sprung up in this space, but from different angles in his backyard you can still see the meeting and its characteristically unimposing Quaker cemetery, where Edward is buried.

And just as many outsider artists are fully part of everyday life, so, too, were many folk artists. Contrary to a lingering sense of them as "starving vagabonds," as the art historian Mary Black put it, folk artists tended to be, she wrote, fairly prosperous. Some of them were also known to the wider world of art. The trained artist John Vanderlyn wrote to a friend that he regretted that (in Mary Black's words) "he had not followed a country career similar to that of Ammi Phillips"—meaning that the folk painter could count on a steady income from an almost unquestioning clientele. Hicks's *Peaceable Kingdoms* and even his historical pictures, however, were not products of a country career. Traditional folk art was as much a service and a business as an art form. It provided inexpensive versions of portraits, landscapes, sculptural busts, and figurines for the mantel to a rural audience that couldn't afford, or maybe didn't even know of, the versions created in metropolitan centers. This is hardly the genesis of Hicks's easel paintings.

More significantly, we perceive the Kingdoms, I think, in something of the way we do works by outsiders. Taking in a folk art portrait or landscape, or a carved wood eagle, we almost invariably register a degree of ineptitude, which is made up for by energy, charm, and, at times, audacity. Taking in, on the other hand, an elaborate presentation of an alternative world by Ramírez or Darger—or quilts composed of an unorthodox blending of abstract shapes made by Mary Lee Bendolph—we are unconcerned with artistic skill. We don't (as we do with folk art) think of the work in relation to how a trained artist could have done the same thing. We are encountering, rather, art in a newly minted, personal language, and this is how we absorb the Kingdoms.

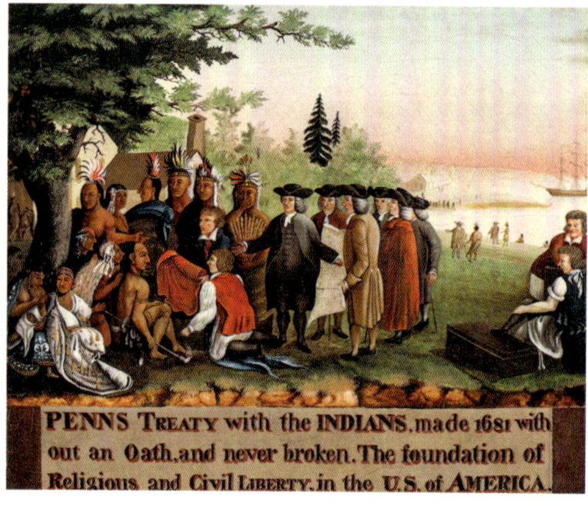

Edward Hicks, *Penn's Treaty with the Indians*, 1840–45, 25 × 30 1/4 in. (63.5 × 76.8 cm).

• • •

YET THERE UNDENIABLY is a degree of ineptitude in Hicks's work. It isn't felt (or it isn't felt strongly) when we look at his Kingdoms because his drawing and painting of animals gives them a physicality and a sense of volume, and of character, that whisks them—unlike the flatter, more decorative and impersonal jungle creatures of Henri Rousseau—to a realm of corporeal believability. Hicks's principal animals have the same multi-dimensional life that the human subjects of great portraits have. But when he handles human anatomy Hicks is not believable in the same way. Here, he is a folk artist.

Working, we presume, intuitively, "little-tutored and self-taught" painters, as Black put it, tend to make figures that are generally squat, though with some artists (especially when presenting soldiers in formation), the figures are matchstick-thin. Hicks is of the squat school. When he paints people, his figures generally have roughly the same waddling presence and cartoon face. Eyes are merely, inertly, black disks.

The small, faraway groups of Quakers and Native Americans in Hicks's Kingdoms are primitive-art creations on this order. Even more so are his paintings of historical events—whether of Penn's treaty, Washington's crossing, or the Declaration signing—which are populated primarily by people. These pictures can hold our attention simply as objects; the color in the paintings of the dumpy and innocuous Penn winning over the Lenni Lanape can be marvelous. But Hicks is successful with these historical scenes primarily when he makes titles or descriptions of the event part of the canvases. When he set words and dates, rendered in classically elegant (Caslon) lettering, in a band across the bottom or right over the top of his picture, the band and words become part of the image—and the painting becomes less flatly and literally about its story. It becomes more an emblem of a historical event, not simply a guileless recreation of it (and the crudeness in the drawing of the figures is less apparent).

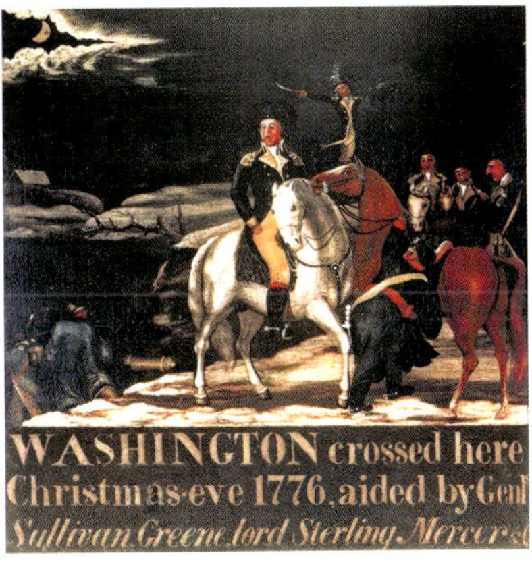

Edward Hicks, *Washington Crossing the Delaware*, 1833, 31 ½ × 31 ½ in. (80 × 80 cm).

The idea of including words undoubtedly came from the fact that Hicks took commissions for signs. This was the origin of his two 1834 versions of Washington at the Delaware. (One hung on the New Jersey side of a bridge spanning the river, one on the Pennsylvania side.) Maybe because he knew his image would need to have an impact from afar, Hicks worked with a brusque forcefulness, and the version of this bridge marker in the Mercer Museum is one of his more powerful pictures. It is predominately

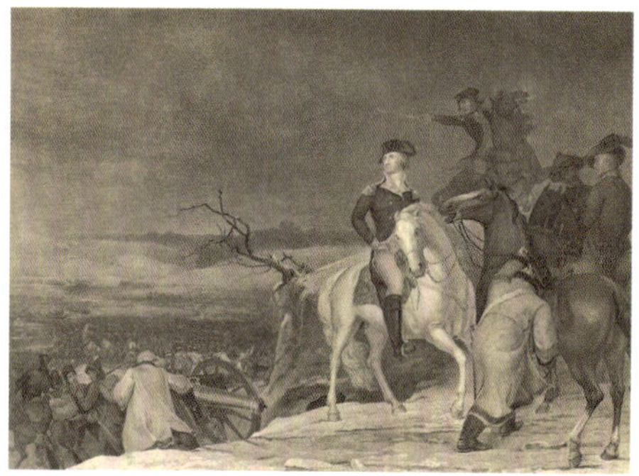

George S. Lang, *Washington Passing the Delaware,* 1825.

in black, white, and a nicely washed-out yellow, with a generously-sized band at the bottom, for the words and dates describing the scene. The beautiful mixture of capital and lowercase letters, and numbers and italics, gives the picture its extra tensile strength. His roughly half-dozen other versions, which are generally on canvas, not wood board, and do not have words or dates, are somewhat dormant attempts to re-do the (somewhat dormant) painting by Thomas Sully from 1819 that was his model.

Unlike Sully, and unlike Emanuel Leutze in his well-known *Washington Crossing the Delaware,* from 1851, Hicks, in his punchy, signboard version, has emphasized the darkness of the moment. The sky is black, slit open at the top by clouds to present the moon. It would be exciting to see Hicks's picture, which is a little less than three feet on a side, in a room with Sully's canvas, which measures twelve by seventeen feet, and Leutze's picture, weighing in at twelve by twenty-one feet. It is very likely that Hicks's rousing, juicily painted version, with the general's face merely sketched in (his eyes seem crossed), would seem much fresher to viewers than its two inexpressive and self-important mates.

One might wonder whether Hicks wasn't fundamentally a sign painter, with the *Peaceable Kingdoms* being signs done for himself. The swiftly drawn black outlines sometimes evident around the bodies of the lion or ox, which no doubt make these shapes stand out more, could derive from the thinking of a sign painter. Seeing them in this light, however, doesn't alter their power. In the same way that every fine-art painting isn't profound, every sign isn't superficial. Besides, in Hicks's finest Kingdoms the delicacy and sparkling clarity of the shapes and details, down to the wheat that the formerly carnivorous lion holds in his mouth, is what makes the work magnetic, and such precision has little to do with sign painting.

• • •

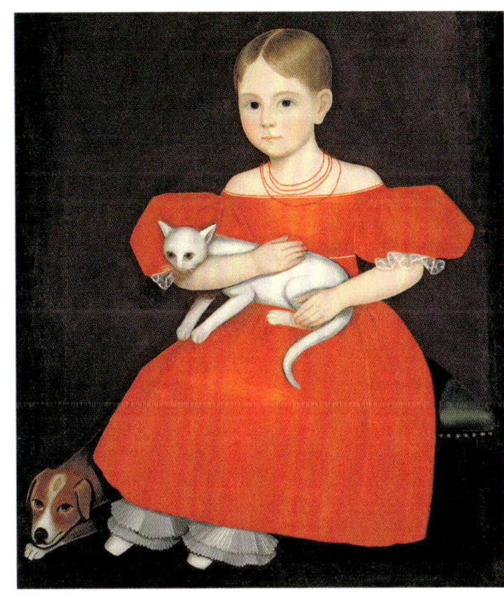

Ammi Phillips, *Girl in a Red Dress with Cat and Dog*, 1830–35, 30 × 25 in. (76.2 × 63.5 cm).

IT IS SURPRISING, though, how few primitive or naive artists are as substantial as Hicks. There are, of course, numerous portraits, townscapes, fanciful scenes, and mourning pictures by such artists—and objects including weathervanes and toys, or the highly realistic painted wood sculptures by the short-lived Asa Ames—that continue to please us. It is rare, though, to find that self-taught or naive artists whose works do hold our attention have made more than a handful of such successes. Very few folk painters left, like Hicks, pictures in number that are also works of such refinement or vigor that we want to keep seeing more of them.

Sheldon Peck is a figure to include in this company. The nervous intensity in the eyes and the taut, almost translucent skin of the portrait subjects of this still sketchily known, Illinois-based painter recall Otto Dix and the early Lucian Freud. The better-known portraitist Ammi Phillips, who sometimes shows his sitters subtly leaning, is, in his feeling for shape and color—for the way one color permeates another—one of the more sheerly elegant painters that the country ever produced. And Jacob Maentel, who has remained a name primarily for folk-art experts—in part because his works are watercolors on paper, which means that museums cannot have them prominently displayed for long—made full-length portraits, but in small sizes, of people who, beguilingly, are seen in the places they lived or worked.

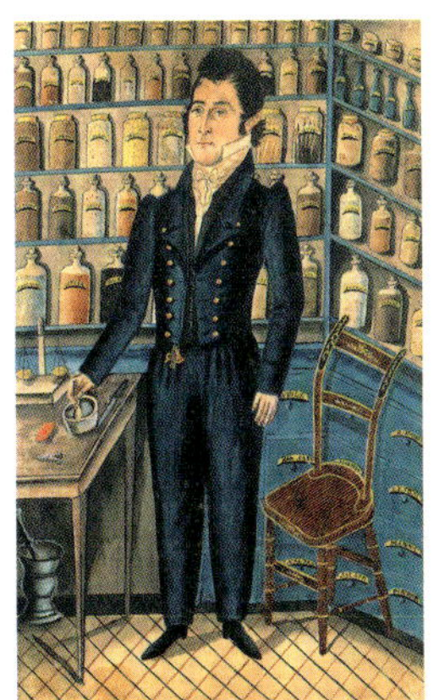

Jacob Maentel, *Dr. Christian Bucher*, c. 1825–30, 16 ½ × 10 ½ in. (41.9 × 26.7 cm).

The marine and landscape (and British-born) painter Thomas Chambers, meanwhile, who in recent years was finally accorded a serious, full museum retrospective—and whose *Niagara Falls* has already been mentioned—is, like Hicks, a figure who makes the term folk artist seem insufficient.

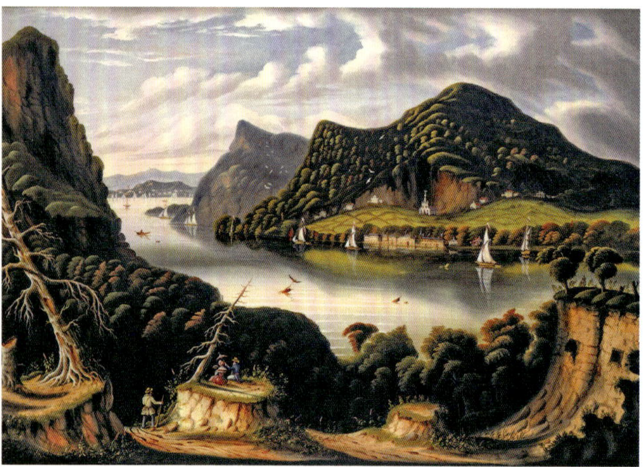

Thomas Chambers, *View of Cold Spring and Mount Taurus from Fort Putnam*, 1845–55, 42 5/8 × 58 in. (108.4 × 147.3 cm).

His harbors with sailing ships, riverside terrains, forested hills, and cloud-filled skies are so freely and invigoratingly drawn and colored that our first response to them is simply to smile. For some of us he is the most charged and embraceable of all American view painters of the time—which is saying something as landscapes (and marines to a lesser extent) were the foremost product of professional, mainstream American artists in the middle decades of the nineteenth century. I may not be alone in getting more pleasure from a picture by Chambers than from most of the efforts of Thomas Cole, Asher Durand, or Frederic Church, traditional artists in every sense.

And the New York City–based James Bard, who initially co-authored his works with his twin brother John, made the painting of steamboats a surprising delight. These good-sized pictures (roughly four feet across is typical) are reliably of spotlessly new vessels, shown from the starboard side. They are, in a sense, advertisements for the builders, owners, or captains of the boats, who sometimes commissioned the works, and, after you have seen two or three, they ought to become monotonous. They are fundamentally little different from series made by other artists of champion horses.

But some combination of the excitement of steamboats themselves and the artistry of James Bard elevated these pictures. With practically each example, he involves us anew in his slightly different presentation of the ship machinery and intricately detailed and colored woodwork on the decks of the vessels—and in the never-quite-the-same handling of clouds, water currents, landscape backgrounds, and spray as the boats push their way along. The decks are usually starkly empty but for a number of stiffly drawn little men, invariably outfitted in black suits and black stovepipe hats, whose placement would appear to be random or decorative (although two of them, in the painting *John Birbeck*, are, puzzlingly, involved in a fistfight). Their presence, coming on top of all the many other precise little details that our eyes want to eat up, is what makes Bard utterly distinctive.

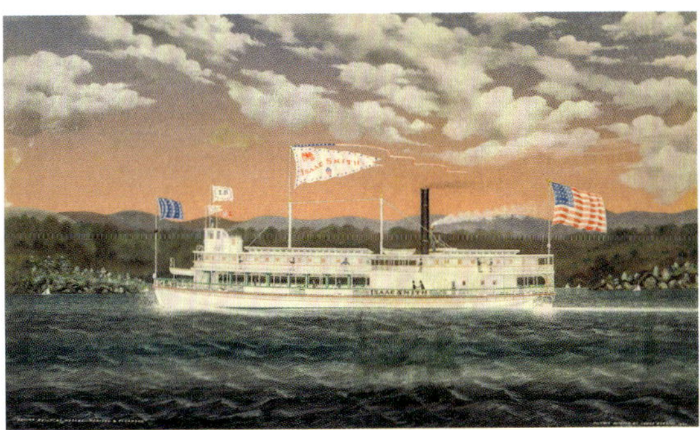

James Bard, *The Steamboat "Isaac Smith" on the Hudson River*, 1861, 31 × 52 in. (78.7 × 132 cm).

But with none of these artists do we follow from picture to picture, as we do with Hicks, the permutations of an idea, or the development of a style. Or as David Tatham put it, there is "organic growth" to Hicks's pictures as we go through them chronologically—and such growth is "absent in the work of most folk painters who like Peter Pan never grow older." Although Ammi Phillips had an early and a later approach, he never went beyond the confines of portraiture. Bard deviated from steamboats only to do sailboats. And Chambers, for all the dash and vigor he brought to it, was always a view painter.

• • •

A SELF-TAUGHT PAINTER whose images did change over time is Erastus Salisbury Field, and for this, and because he also derived subjects from the Bible—and wanted to acknowledge, in his work, being American—he is the artist most linked with Hicks. Field is a kind of Hicks without the pressing need to send a message (or without the inner steel). As objects on the wall, Field's pictures cannot match those of Hicks, either. With his muzzy painter's touch, Field's canvases lack the polish, oomph, and feeling for strong color that Hicks regularly had on hand. Field was fanatical in his gentler way, however, and his body of work has venturesome twists and intriguing near-successes.

A native of central Massachusetts, he began as a portraitist, and while he wasn't as incisive as Peck or as suave as Phillips, his generally good-sized portraits have a style of their own. In their Sunday-best clothes, with only hints of expression on their intelligent, often severe but sometimes wry faces, Field's sitters, who are sometimes seen in such a way that their heads are at the top of otherwise primarily darkened spaces, have justifiably and astutely been called "looming giants" and "provincial royalty."

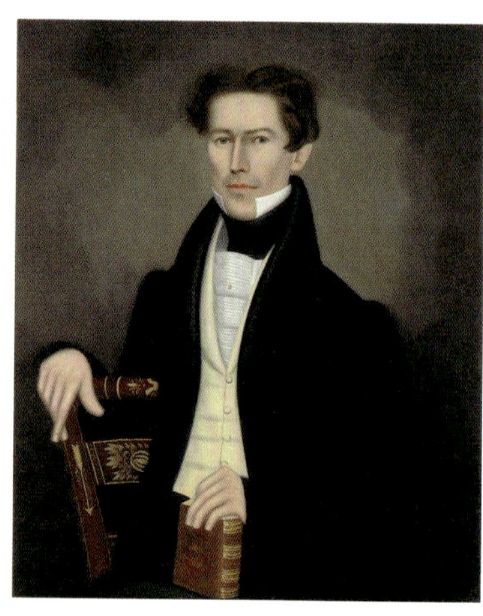

Erastus Salisbury Field, *Charles Backus Jones*, c. 1833, 35 7/16 × 29 7/16 in. (90 × 74.7 cm).

After the daguerreotype put a hole in the painted portrait business, Field began making portraits that seem to blend, lugubriously and a little nightmarishly, painting and photography. Ultra-realistic concoctions of this sort, which might bring together Lincoln and his generals (with Washington thrown in), represent the artist at his wackiest. He pulled out all his stops, however, for his *Historical Monument of the American Republic*, a painting that measures nine feet high by thirteen feet across and was worked on in spurts from 1867 to 1888. It presents a miragelike scene of interconnected temples that are so huge that the human beings that we see here and there can seem, before we get close to the picture, like ants.

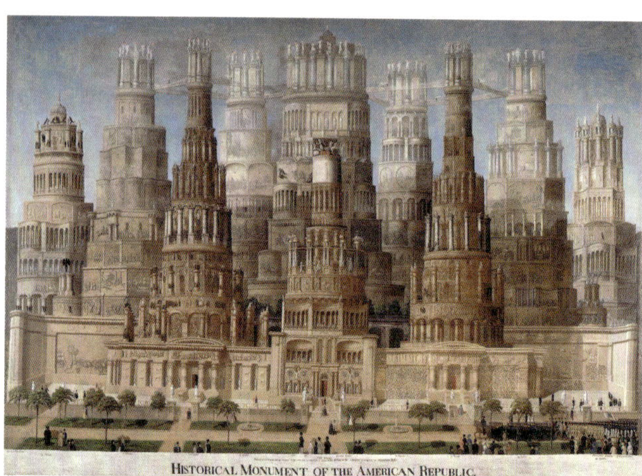

Erastus Salisbury Field, *Historical Monument of the American Republic*, 1867–88, 111 × 157 in. (281.9 × 398.8 cm).

What is alive about the painting is less Field's synthesis of America's past than the heroically painstaking and ingenuous way he went about it. With its zones of text and its countless images that seem to emanate from the temple walls—and its ominous lettering, portentous numbers, Biblical references, and so forth—the work is like a cross between a map and a graphic novel. If Field's desire to celebrate America pegs the picture to nineteenth-century folk art, his wild ambition and chartlike approach give the canvas something of the mixture of grandiosity and mysterious thought patterns seen in works of some outsider artists.

Field's *Monument* has been beautifully summed up by E. P. Richardson as "an architectural fantasy so strange, so ingenious, so labored and absurd that it succeeds in expressing, with a genuine and touching eloquence, the love and visions of grandeur that filled his simple mind." We are less likely nowadays to write, as Richardson did in the mid-1950s (in his often first-rate *Painting in America*), that an artist, or anyone, has a "simple mind." Field's art does take us, however—in a way that Hicks in his best work does not—to a rural, closed-in, and innocent America. This is largely felt when human figures (as opposed to portrait subjects) play significant parts in his pictures. Our interest goes slack when confronted with Field's rubbery and goofy approximations of people. Hicks loses us, too, when we face the figures, with their blank, unseeing eyes, in his historical paintings. Yet a note of naivete hangs over Field's art even when human figures are not much in evidence. One senses a childlike tentativeness and docility in the way he fashions many forms.

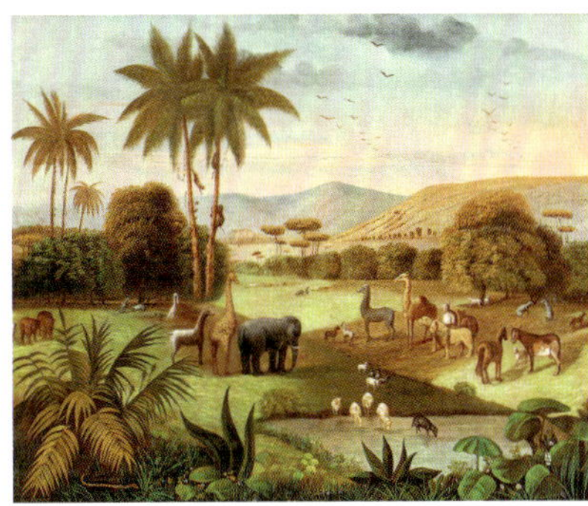

Erastus Salisbury Field, *Garden of Eden*, c. 1860–65, 27 5/8 × 35 in. (69.9 × 88.9 cm).

Field may be seen at his loveliest in his paintings of the Garden of Eden, particularly a version that has come to light in recent years (and is now in the Museum of Fine Arts, in Springfield, Massachusetts). Strangely and luckily, this Garden omits Adam and Eve. Their absence allows us to appreciate uninterruptedly the picture's hazy green and golden light, its varied terrain and waters, and its real and fanciful creatures—headed up by a toylike elephant and a giraffe, who stand like sentinels, facing away from us. This serene work is one of the most endearing of all American paintings.

It might be called a *Peaceable Kingdom* without psychology. What separates Hicks from Field—and from Bard, Phillips, and even the ebullient Chambers—is that their respective universes lack what is felt in the Kingdoms: an ambiguity or tension over what the image is saying to us. Pictures by primitive painters often do have, of course, a dreamlike strangeness, and the stranger ones are among the most memorable and loved of folk paintings. This certainly is the case with canvases in the National Gallery such as Samuel Jordan's *Eaton Family Memorial*, with its tiny horse, huge mourner, and brilliant sky, or the portrait by an unknown artist from about 1790 of Dr. Philemon Tracy, where the doctor, holding the outstretched wrist of someone we do not otherwise see, looks out at us.

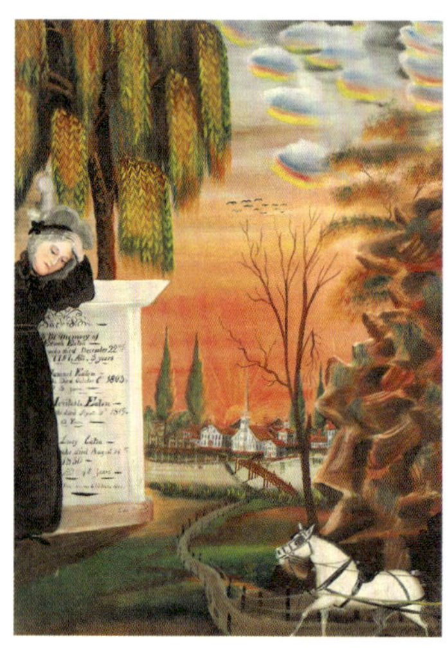

Samuel Jordan, *Eaton Family Memorial*, 1831, 21 7/8 × 15 1/2 in. (55.6 × 39.4 cm).

Paintings like these (and the National Gallery's collection has a number of them) make understandable how naive pictures, in the 1930s and into the 1940s, when they were coming into their own, were thought by some to anticipate Surrealism, then in its heyday. Such works could be particularly appealing to the Surrealists themselves, because they were like the found objects—the troubling, random, from-nowhere oddities—that they prized. Pictures such as Samuel Jordan's mourning scene could be taken as a prod to stir up the unconscious.

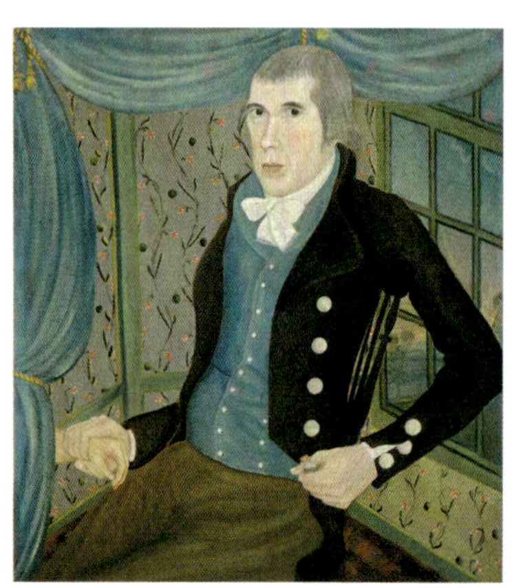

Unknown American artist, *Dr. Philemon Tracy*, c. 1790, 31 1/8 × 28 7/8 in. (79.1 × 73.4 cm).

The Kingdoms, however, are not ad hoc oddities. They have their own inner logic. They present hopes and wishes, which are uncertainties, and uncertainty pervades the scenes. Like many a call for peace, they imply, or are equally about, conflict. We look at scenes that in the next instant could be massacres. The underlying precariousness of feeling of the Kingdoms is heard in a comment, which slightly mangles Isaiah's prophesy, about unusually warm weather in December that appeared in an article in *The New York Times*. There Mr. Abe Shoener, a winemaker, was recorded as saying, "Maybe it's the kind of wonderful thing where the lamb lies down with the lion, but maybe it is the end of the world."

• • •

THAT THE KINGDOMS embody uncertainty and expectation as much as peace (or any settled state) is—possibly—borne out by the work of another artist. This is Martin Johnson Heade, Hicks's onetime shop assistant, who, I believe, was thinking of the older painter's canvases when he made his own pictures about disquietude. After Heade left Bucks County he eventually became a landscapist, and he hit his stride in the 1860s with a handful of masterful pictures of coming storms which convey the dread of such moments with unnerving accuracy. In the 1870s, he pursued the same ominous mood more indirectly with images of orchids in full bloom in misty mountainous tropical settings, with a hummingbird or two perched nearby.

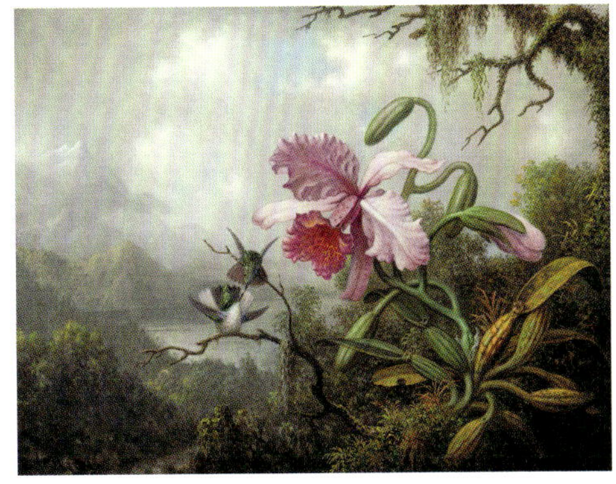

Martin Johnson Heade, *Orchid and Hummingbirds Near a Mountain Lake*, c. 1875–90, 15 3⁄16 × 20 1⁄2 in. (38.6 × 52.1 cm).

Although the birds and the plants are not, of course, connecting with one another, the image Heade devised has the spirit of a tango. Rearing up on its powerful curving stem in the direction of the tiny birds—both the plant and the hummingbirds are seen in their actual sizes—the looming orchid appears to be offering its sexualized self to them. (Heade's explicitness about the orchid's wide-opened genital presence remains startling.) The plant might be getting ready to devour the birds.

Heade's pictures, which are unlike anything in American art (or art), are thought to be inventions on his part. Yet, surely, they echo the *Peaceable Kingdoms* he knew from Newtown. I may be alone among writers on the two painters in seeing a link, but I find it irresistible. The structures of Heade's and of Hicks's scenes are the same: plants or animals are seen right at the lip of crowded, small stages, with a landscape behind them. And we look at scenes that suggest aggression or the craving of one participant for the other—here momentarily suspended. Heade was making amoral Kingdoms.

Yet the largest difference between the Kingdoms and folk art may be that in Hicks's pictures we feel him personally. We are given a sense of an artist's inner life in a way that isn't there even in the work of many professional American painters of the time. Hicks didn't comment on the matter directly. But in a sermon he gave in the late 1830s, where he described the psychological makeup of the different animals, he saw the lion as emblematic of those who live on a short fuse and are quick to become arrogant and angry. They are prone to "become leaders of the people (for leaders they will be)." He knew that it was his own nature to be vituperative, superior, and intolerant. In the sermon and elsewhere, he hung his head in remorse about it.

Does this mean that in the lion Hicks was picturing himself? He would, I think, reject the idea in principle. Covertly including himself in the scenes would be impious. As a Quaker, he believed that the very point of the wild, carnivorous beasts commingling with their tame prey is to show that the lion, the wolf, the bear, and the leopard have learned to give up their self-regard. It could be said that the Kingdoms are about the defeat of self-regard and the victory of a selfless innocence, represented by the farm animals. But just as an arrived-at peace can suggest strife, selflessness can make us think of its opposite.

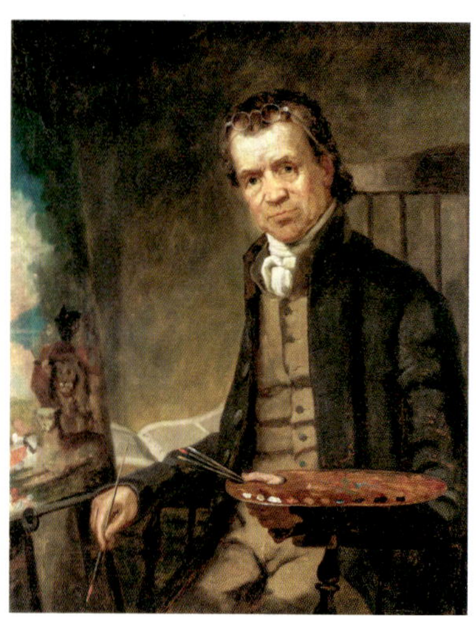

Thomas Hicks, *Portrait of Edward Hicks*, 1838–41, 27 1/4 × 22 1/8 in. (69.2 × 56.2 cm).

The lion does, after all, have a human face—Hicks was hardly the first artist to make this apparent—and the similarity of the cat's and the artist's visage has been remarked on. It can be checked in the one image we have of Hicks, an oil portrait by his cousin Thomas (who made a few versions of the work). In the painting,

Edward, then about sixty, does, if loosely, resemble the lion. Edward had sustained a broken nose, and his resulting slightly flattened look could pass for leonine. It is hard not to think that, as he made *Peaceable Kingdoms* again and again, and kept changing the appearance and expression of the lion, he was describing something of his own evolution. Perhaps he returned to the subject repeatedly because it gave him this chance—as if the subject were his own private mirror.

To follow the lion's changes of bearing chronologically (which is possible in an approximate way, even though so many of the pictures are undated), is to get a convincing, naturalistic record of aging. The lion goes from being, in the early Kingdoms of the 1820s, a kind of shy, doglike cat, to becoming, roughly in the next decade, a vigilant and physically commanding but uncomfortable being. Pictures from the 1840s show him as a benign ruler, or, slipping in his authority, as merely a spectator of the leopard's prowess—even a companion, as fellow seniors, of the massive ox. In other late examples, he can appear distraught, or merely befuddled.

Although the overall story being presented could belong to anyone, Hicks's presentation of it is unique and unexpected. It forms a sort of autobiography, and it is as engaging, moving, and purely visual a one as any conceived by an American artist. Yet it would limit the *Peaceable Kingdoms* to believe that the story they are telling is about the lion. A number of writers on Hicks (and others who know the Kingdoms well) are certain that the artist saw himself in the leopard. Perhaps the two cats are two sides of the same being: one prey to time and thought, the other pure sentience. But both creatures have their fullest meaning when they are seen as part of an assembly, or family—the subject, one feels, that meant the most to Hicks.

The Families

I HAVE WAITED to mention Hicks's life as a Quaker until after giving a sense of his art because it is as an artist that most of us come to know him and that he remains alive. His work can be loved without a viewer knowing very much about Quakerism. Yet Hicks's religiosity, and the conflicts he faced as a member of the Society of Friends, and the tension incurred over being a Quaker and an artist, enriched his art. It led to the backbone of his work as a painter: his exploring the prophesy in Isaiah. There is, moreover, something amazing, or at the least uncanny, about the conjunction of Hicks—with his particular background and upbringing, his singular gifts as an artist, and his wildly fertile faultfinding imagination—and his being a Quaker at that precise time.

Hicks was more than devout. He appears to have been almost infatuated with Quakerism. The Society of Friends had been around for close to two centuries when he became an established figure in it, but little of its story, whether concerning its thinking, history, or heroes, seems to have felt like the past to him. "To-day I think I have been edified and encouraged," he noted in his diary in the 1840s, "in reading two of dear William Penn's sermons, preached more than one hundred and fifty years ago."

The Religious Society of Friends was founded in England by George Fox, who sought a form of worship, of drawing closer to God, that would dispense with the rituals and organizational hierarchies that established religions operated under but which he believed took on a life of their own—a life that pulled one away from Christ's message. Fox's thinking didn't come out of the blue. It was part of the same upheaval among Protestants in England in the seventeenth century that saw Puritans leaving England for the Massachusetts Bay Colony for their religious freedom and that gave birth twenty years later, in the 1650s, to the Puritan Revolution that saw King Charles I beheaded and Oliver Cromwell made Lord Protector. It was the upheaval that witnessed the rise of Presbyterianism, Methodism, Congregationalism, Baptism, and other forms of worship. These developments were all in their way about achieving a more genuine sense of religious communion than that laid down by the Established, or Anglican, Church. The Society of Friends stood at the extreme edge, or the furthest left, of these reforming developments.

Fox himself was fervent and mystical. When called before a magistrate who questioned his thinking, Fox answered that even the judge "must tremble and quake at the Word of the Lord." The judge apparently asked Fox if he were a quaker, and thus the appellation was born. It stuck because the word suggests the faith's otherworldly and nonconformist roots. It captures the religion's physicality: its belief that what Fox called the Inner Light, which cannot easily be summarized, and, roughly, is about being taken outside one's self—and being flooded with a sense of the Truth—is felt first in the body. The theatricality implied by such bodily awareness, with the attendant visionary moments that early Quakers had, also helps explain the hounding and accusations of witchcraft they suffered, especially in the seventeenth century.

Quakers believed in the ability of each congregant to worship on her or his own, without the aid of intermediaries. Although, in time, the roles of elders and ministers developed, there was no profession of officiating person—no priests, pastors, or fathers. There were no creeds, either, or prayer books, hymns, or the music to accompany them. The Bible did remain a crucial guide. (The middle of the seventeenth century was when Bibles were widely disseminated for the first time.) But although Bible stories were part of Quaker Sunday School, the book was not used in adult worship. No book was.

• • •

Perhaps the most radical aspect of Quaker thinking was the silent meeting for worship. It still feels radical. It can be seen as the greatest

Quaker invention. People came together for a set time—as they continue to do so today—and sat. No one was assigned to speak, and an hour could go by without anyone's uttering a word. If you needed to speak you did.

You were there, in an actual and a metaphoric sense—to use a verb that cannot be bettered—to wait. What you waited for, ideally, was to be filled with the Inner Light, which is also referred to as the Inward Light, the Light Within, or simply the Light. The similarity with classic psychoanalysis—with the hour spent on one's back, not looking at one's psychiatrist, waiting for whatever might spring forth—is remarkable. Equally noteworthy, as Howard H. Brinton put it in his invaluable *Friends for 350 Years*, is the similarity of the Quaker meeting for worship with Zen meditation, conducted in a group. The difference is that the meeting for worship is not intended to be about the single person having a personal thought. It is, rather, about the group itself. The hope is that congregants will speak, and not about themselves. Intuitively coming to a sense of the Inner Light means you are brought closer simultaneously to God and to your connectedness to all people. In Quaker thinking, it can seem as if there is little difference between the two.

Quaker belief that there should be no hierarchy among people as they approached God, and that it was the group itself that was waiting for God, or Truth, led with some logic to the conviction that it was a Quaker responsibility to work for the betterment of all people here and now. As Brinton put it, in a meeting for worship there is "no screen of words and abstract concepts between the soul and reality"—reality having the same weight as the soul. The name "Society of Friends," which came in date a little after the word "Quaker," clearly suggests an organization that is of this world and is about equality, responsibility, and permeability.

In their reforming quest, Friends seemed to want to start the world anew, and they were obdurate. In their first many decades, their beliefs kept them susceptible to jail terms, particularly in England, where they were barred from universities and from holding public office. They didn't believe in swearing, hence they refused to take oaths. They pointed to admonitions not to swear in the New Testament. The implication of swearing to tell the whole truth in court, Quakers believed, was that one did not speak in full truthfulness when not sworn in—an untenable position. Combined with their abhorrence of conflict, this belief in not swearing about anything resulted in a refusal to serve in the military. (Pacifists during the American Revolution, they were able to pass through zones held by the British and the colonists.)

Words, or how things are known, were seen by Quakers to need revamping as well. They elevated to a central position in their lexicon the marvelously neutral, everyday, and functional word "meeting." It became their word for church. They had meetinghouses, not churches. They went "to meeting" as Christians go "to church" or Jews go "to temple." Troubled by the pagan origin of the names for the months and for the week, Friends got rid of September, Tuesday, and all the rest. Instead they noted what they did (in letters or in the journals many of them kept) on, say, 1st 19th (or 19 d). (Sunday was First day.) Edward Hicks, for example, might write that he was born on 4th mo 4th, 1780.

Quakers understandably emphasized equality in all things—among all men, of course, and among men and women. Women or men served as ministers, and, at least in Hicks's day, women, particularly English Friends, were major spokespersons for one proposal or another (though this didn't mean that power plays between men and women were erased—or, as Edward put it in his memoirs, it was of "great importance of superior women always being right, for when they get wrong they are so difficult to manage"). Friends used "thee" and "thou" instead of "you"—Herman Melville referred to "the stately dramatic thee and thou of the Quaker idiom"—because usage had elevated "you" to a position implying power over one, and Friends saw this as a denial of equality. For them using "you" was like when we add the supposedly deferential and essentially phony "sir" in addressing someone.

They refused to use the prefix "Saint," too, even when it was part of a place name. That was just more insincere lip service to a superiority Quakers (and most of the rest of us) do not believe in. They rejected the societal norm of the time of doffing one's hat: it is a sign of respect, and Friends (amusingly belying their name) saw such shows of indiscriminate respect as an imposture. You did not truly feel that the person you took your hat off to was superior to you. Thus in images of Quakers, including those by Edward Hicks, they are often wearing hats.

The most notable instances of the Society's insistence on equality were in their efforts over time to deal with respect to those Native Americans they came in contact with and, more significantly, in their century-long quest to break up slavery. (They opposed capital punishment as well.) George Fox saw the iniquity of slave owning already in the middle of the seventeenth century, and eventually, wrote Alfred North Whitehead, Quakers "gave the first modern formulation of an explicit purpose to procure the abolition of slavery." Convincing all Friends to participate in the relinquishing of slaves and not purchasing new ones took, however, painstaking, incremental persuasion. The illustrious Friend William Penn, for example, who in 1682 was given the land that would become Pennsylvania from the King—in payment for what the Crown owed Penn's father—and who along the way had been, as a young man, imprisoned for his Quaker beliefs, owned slaves. But in 1774 the Society officially condemned slavery.

It was Quakers in the eighteenth century, wrote Garry Wills in his *Head and Heart: American Christianities*, who provided the real impetus for the abolitionism that took wing in the nineteenth century. In the writings and ministry of John Woolman and in the efforts of Anthony Benezet, who ran a free school in Philadelphia for poor black children and whose writings on the subject had an audience even in France and Germany, the arguments used to justify slavery, particularly the belief that it was sanctioned in the Bible—a key justification for slaveholders—were shown to be unreasonable, fallacious, and immoral. Benezet, we read, "made himself an international clearinghouse for information about slavery and for agitation against it." In Wills's comprehensive study of some 550 pages, the chapter on Quakers is but seventeen pages long. But *Head and Heart* is dedicated solely to Anthony Benezet.

• • •

An ambiguity inherent in Quakerism is that while in principle it ruled out traditional religious hierarchies, it needed an organizational system of its own or it would collapse. What the Society evolved was a kind of governing web. In addition to the weekly meeting for worship, there were Monthly, Quarterly, and Yearly meetings, and meetings on the local level for business and for "sufferings," which meant attending to people who needed help of any kind. Meetings sprang up when there were sufficient numbers of persons to justify such an entity, and a Quarterly meeting would have represented in it more jurisdictions than a Monthly meeting. A Yearly meeting would be bigger still. In accordance with the emphasis on the group, not the individual, decisions were generally not made by vote but by a "sense" of the group's feelings. The outcome of a vote—in any circumstance—would, further, mean that one side "won," or represented the majority, and while there actually were votes in this or that meeting, the notion of winners and losers was in principle anathema in the Society of Friends.

And while there was no priest class, each meeting would have elders, who in turn appointed ministers. Neither were paid. Elders, who first became part of Quaker life in 1714, were meant to guard, check, prod, and support ministers. They formed a kind of balancing act with ministers; and in the protective, watchful way that the ox, in a *Peaceable Kingdom*, practically shelters the lion Hicks could very well be enacting the relationship of the elder and the minister. The ox literally has the lion's back.

People were asked to be ministers who could and did speak forth; but they didn't go to meeting with the assumption that they would necessarily address their fellows, nor did they write out their thoughts beforehand (or at least they were not supposed to). Speaking at a meeting for worship was extemporaneous or it was nothing. Even coming to meeting with some nuggets culled from the Bible, to be sprinkled in, was frowned on, at least by Edward Hicks, always ready to pounce on a showy Friend. His own sermons were not written out beforehand. That we have some of them comes in part from the fact that there was a stenographer in the room. And that Edward in his sermons quoted Bible passages at length bespeaks his working familiarity with the book. We know that from the 1650s or so, people of all denominations committed goodly amounts of the Bible to memory.

Ministers had lives and occupations quite separate from their meeting. But as ministers they might—as Edward did—visit the sick, attend the dying, and speak at funerals. He also dug the graves. His cousin Elias Hicks, who was also a minister—a more widely renowned one than Edward—was a carpenter by trade (and a farmer as well) who helped erect his meetinghouse in Jericho, on Long Island; and ministers were expected to maintain the meetinghouse. Edward received ten dollars a year to sweep and clean the Newtown Meeting and make fires for it in the cold months (and from that ten, he noted, a dollar to two went for "the contingent expenses"). It is because of this duty that one sometimes sees him referred to as his meeting's "janitor."

It was also expected, or hoped, of ministers that they would travel, to address their fellows or even non-Quakers. Up through the first two-thirds of the nineteenth century (or before the railroad changed American life), ministers, accompanied often by elders, put up with the most arduous conditions as they made their way on horseback, often through unknown terrain, attending meetings as they found them. Edward, on separate trips, got as far as Canada, Virginia, and Ohio. His spirited nephew Edward Hicks Kennedy, who became a doctor, wrote in 1830 from St. Louis to his cousin Elizabeth Hicks that his uncle Edward was known even in Missouri. Young Edward had been talking with an older woman about a local issue when she suddenly wondered, "What would *Mr. Hicks* say to such manoeuvres?" Just to be sure she wasn't meaning Elias, of Long Island, Kennedy asked which Hicks, and heard "why the famous Quaker preacher in Pennsylvania!"

In an America where new Christian sects bubbled up seemingly every month, and people regularly sampled preachers of any and all denominations, Edward's name preceded him, and not only in Quaker circles. Elias called Edward's ministerial gift "searching and lively," and this tallies with the rough sense we have from accounts, chiefly in Alice Ford's biography, of Edward's preaching. It seems to have veered from lengthy and stern immersions in the Scriptures to engaging metaphors and trenchant jabs addressing everyday, or usually Quaker, foibles. (Liveliness is lacking in the few sermons of his that were published. They feel padded.)

Quakers through much of the eighteenth and into the nineteenth century, especially in America, could feel themselves linked, not only as a faith and a family but almost as a political party. They were significant players in business and governing life in Pennsylvania in particular, at least in the first half of the 1700s, and they had a presence along the coast from Rhode Island to North Carolina. (How could they serve in government without taking an oath? Through "affirmation," a formal agreement that involved no swearing.) Quakers at one time essentially ran the thriving port of Philadelphia, the country's premier city, and for a century and a half they controlled the whaling industry in Nantucket and New Bedford, which meant serious money in an age in need of whale oil. Readers of *Moby-Dick* will remember that Captain Bildad and Captain Peleg, who are Quaker, were the principal owners of the *Pequod*.

The assurance of Friends in business touched Edward Hicks directly. His New York merchant cousins, Isaac and Samuel Hicks, both helped generously when Edward, in his thirties—and not at all close then to either relative—got himself into serious financial straits as he attempted to be a farmer. A figure of considerable importance in his time, Isaac had turned himself by the early years of the 1800s into the preeminent shipowner in New York City. A boat of his called the *Sally Hicks* was long referred to as the "Queen of the Whaling Fleet." Yet Isaac's life as a Quaker had an equal hold on him. He accompanied his cousin Elias on at least four of his ministerial trips, and Isaac's significant library, in his Westbury, Long Island home, was a resource that Elias, in his writing, regularly counted on.

Yet another well-to-do New York City merchant cousin, Henry Hicks (Samuel's son), came to Edward's aid in his last years and then posthumously. It was Henry who paid to have important sermons of Edward's printed and distributed free of charge, and although Edward died before his *Memoirs* was published, he knew that Henry would foot this bill as well.

• • •

QUAKER SELF-AWARENESS had grown greatly with the advent, in the 1700s, of a spirit—it was in no way a movement—called quietism. Many of the scruples and strictures about behavior and language that have already been noted—the thinking that set Quakers apart—might be labelled quietist. The term bears out an insight of the twentieth-century spiritualist and lecturer Gerald Heard. In Eleanore Price Mather's *Pendle Hill: A Quaker Experiment in Education and Community*, she quotes Heard as saying that the "main problem of Quakerism may be comprised into a phrase—a religious body which, advisedly, refused to have a theology must at some time create a psychology or it will mislay its essential discoveries." Quietism in a sense was that "psychology."

The connotations of the word "quietism" are not liberating, and some Quaker mores of the time, which stressed Quaker purity and exclusivity, are off-putting. In the need to maintain their particular identity, Friends created schools—for the children of Friends. Disownments from a meeting, always an aspect of the faith, were now ramped up. Betsy Ross, who came from a Quaker family in Philadelphia and is thought to have made one of the earliest American flags, was disowned by her meeting—this was a few years before the flag—for marrying outside the Society. For some congregations you couldn't even attend a wedding if it wasn't a Quaker wedding. Abstemious and ascetic proclivities even influenced clothing. The era of Quaker "drab"—i. e., a color more nebulous and pointedly neutral than mere gray—was at hand. When we meet Captain Bildad in the early pages of *Moby-Dick,* his "drab vesture was buttoned up to his chin" and for good measure he looked at you with a "drab-colored eye."

Yet the quietist era also saw an emphasis on both the mystical nature of the faith and on the seemingly different realization that social activism was a property of Quakerism. Anthony Benezet and John Woolman, whose *Journal* may be the most acclaimed piece of writing by a Quaker of any era, subscribed to quietist thinking, and so did Elias and Edward Hicks a generation or two later. In time the different impulses within Quakerism—its pulls toward and against a separate path—would make for serious fissures.

But even as the Society of Friends was losing its complex unity, Quakers could strike outside observers, in England as much as in America, as stirringly, even romantically, distinctive. For Charles Lamb, writing in 1821 about a meeting for worship in London, the "very garments of a Quaker seem incapable of receiving a soil; and cleanliness in them to be something more than the absence of its contrary." Lamb captured maybe as well as anyone the sense of theater afforded by Friends: "When they come up in bands to their Whitsun-conferences, whitening the easterly streets of the metropolis, from all parts of the United Kingdom, they show like troops of the Shining Ones."

• • •

THE RELIGIOUS, ETHICAL, POLITICAL, and social package that was the Society of Friends would strike Edward Hicks, when he was ready for it, as a gift. It seemed tailor-made to feed the religious and disputatious cravings, and to assuage the sense of loss and the anger, he apparently had continually on tap. He came from an established, perhaps even distinguished, New England family that had been on the continent since 1621. That is when Robert Hicks, a London tanner, arrived in the Bay Colony on the *Fortune*, the ship following the *Mayflower*. His descendants included leading judges, delegates to assemblies, and military captains and colonels. They were magistrates and made treaties with Native American tribes. A Hicks had been a Tory mayor of New York City. An uncle of Edward's through marriage, Samuel Seabury, was the first Episcopal bishop in America.

Edward's grandfather Gilbert Hicks, a member by my count of the fifth generation of Hickses in America, was the first of the clan to leave the orbit of New England and Long Island, setting himself up in Pennsylvania, where in time he became chief justice of Bucks County. Gilbert was also a Tory—he was Crown appointed—and he lost his standing and his name during the Revolution. Like some other Loyalists, he eventually escaped to Canada—after periods of hiding in the colonies—and there he died (it is thought assassinated, for his politics). His son Isaac, Edward's father, was a judge as well. Also a Crown appointee and a loyalist, he spent some time during the war, as did his father, in New York City, which was held by the British. The Revolution left this well-placed and well-to-do family—Gilbert's house, we read, was a "mansion," and both he and Isaac owned slaves—financially, socially, and personally wrecked.

Before the war began, Isaac had married, in 1771, Catherine Hicks, a cousin. Two of their children died quite young, but their eldest, Gilbert, growing up in difficult circumstances, landed on his feet: he became a doctor. Their daughter Eliza Violetta (a family name) lived long enough to have three children—we have already briefly met her son Edward Hicks Kennedy—though she died in a water accident in her late thirties. Gilbert and Eliza had the benefit of growing up a little with their mother. This was denied Edward, her last. Catherine, whose spirit seems understandably to have haunted him, died in October 1781, when he was a year and a half old. It was on the 19th, the day Cornwallis surrendered at Yorktown, ending the war, at least on the ground.

Isaac, broke, shunned, and dispirited, was now also a widower with three children. Gilbert and Eliza were found homes to board in, but Edward, not much more than a baby, found himself a home, as it were. It happened one day when he was in the company of a young woman named Jane, who had been one of Catherine's slaves and with whose people he was living. He caught the attention of Elizabeth Twining, a native of Newtown and someone who had known Catherine. She set in motion his coming to live with her and her husband David—and their four nearly all grown daughters—as their foster child. Isaac, who also had some knowledge of David and Elizabeth, must have felt relieved. He gave them an annual sum, and Edward, for the next ten or so years, was a member of the Twining family.

But the child Edward may not have felt entirely settled or secure. His sense of life as being made up of extreme, polar situations, and his heightened awareness of the differences in the rank or standing of people, which is what we see in the assembly of creatures in the *Peaceable Kingdoms*, could have been part of his thinking as he grew up. In his blood was the knowledge that he came from wealth and social distinction. He was literally born in and first lived in Grandfather Gilbert's great house, and both his grandfather and father were addressed as "squire." But before he could walk all that was gone, along with his mother.

Life with the Twinings perpetuated these contrasts. David and Elizabeth were Quakers—Edward's parents were Episcopalians—and David had done extremely well for himself. He maintained the town library at his house, and on the thousand-acre Twining farm in Newtown Edward now had a second chance of being brought up, to use his words, as a "gentleman's son." But David Twining was a strict, dour figure, and he was considerably older than Elizabeth, who apparently supplied in her person and in her feeling for the Bible Edward's chief sources of warmth, sustenance, and learning. He wasn't adopted, and David left him nothing in his will. Nor was he acknowledged years later in the will of Beulah Twining, virtually a sister to Edward and later a good friend, who had become wealthy through her parents' farm and had no children to leave her money to. (In fairness to Beulah, one needs to note that Edward asked her not to be mentioned in her will.)

At age thirteen his bearings were shaken again when his father arranged for him to be indentured to local coachmakers, the Tomilsons. Edward wrote (more than once) that Isaac was "disappointed" in his youngest child's apparently not having the aptitude for professional learning—for the kind of education, in other words, that generations of Hickses had done well by and that his brother Gilbert would demonstrate in becoming a doctor. Isaac could not, his son continued, make a "great man" from "weak little" Edward—who, as it turned out, would be eventually a smallish, lithe but not robust man. He was prone to illness, and he suffered from pulmonary issues.

• • •

IT IS HARD not to feel that many of the prejudices, biases, peeves, obsessions, and bouts of righteous anger, even fury, that—if his memoirs give an accurate account of his temperament—drove the adult Edward, stemmed from the treatment he received from his family. He grew up to be a connoisseur of conflict; he seemingly had a polemical, critical, and partisan angle on every issue he thought worth his attention. He probably would have made a fierce prosecuting attorney and done all the preceding generations of Hickses proud. Actually, he may have been quite like his father and grandfather as they pronounced on cases in their respective courtrooms in that, as a minister, he faced the congregation and spoke from a raised bench. He might have stood and addressed people in meeting more times than his father officiated as a justice of the peace.

Edward didn't, in his autobiographical writing, hold his father to account for anything. Edward's tone is rather neutral when he mentions his father, his grandfather, and his brother Gilbert. In reality, he didn't, as an adult, have a lot to do with Isaac, though they would eventually live not far from each other for decades in the same small town. After the Revolution, Isaac slowly got on his feet again, both as a justice of the peace and as a surveyor. Based in Newtown, and remarried—his second wife, Mary, died in 1812—he laid out many developments in Bucks County. According to Edna S. Pullinger, he was concerned that he was "unable to understand the impracticality and rebelliousness" of Edward, and at one point Isaac bought a little house for his son across the street from his own, but Edward, who had yet to move permanently to Newtown, rejected the offer. Edward seems to have had the same arm's-length relationship with his brother, even though Dr. Gilbert Hicks became not only a Quaker but a minister.

Yet Edward's memoirs read in good part as a many-sided, and sometimes farcically farfetched, fulmination against what the Hicks family had stood for or been associated with: institutional authority; scholastic learning; the British Crown or Englishness in general; doctors; and the ways of any established church. Ranged against these values, which he sometimes calls "aristocratic," are those of the family he became a part of: the Religious Society of Friends.

He didn't put his thoughts together in one graspable brief, and one can feel that his certitudes are based on only adumbrated, flimsy history. But his various arguments form a coherent whole. They fit together ingeniously. What he valued in the Society of Friends was its democratic and egalitarian, and anti-elitist, nature. And like other Quakers drawn to quietism, he was emboldened by a vision of the Christianity of the first century AD—or the thinking and practices of the earliest followers of Christ, who existed prior to the creation of a priest class and the beginning of an organized church.

As Hicks saw it, Quakerism was about "reviving and preserving primitive Christianity." The earliest Christians were almost the first Quakers. The immediate associates of Jesus also worshipped without intermediaries getting between them and their moments of communion with something outside of themselves. But a special wrinkle for Hicks was that these first Christians, conducting themselves as their exemplar did, were carpenters or farmers and believed in manual labor and "humble industry." Hicks saw them as consciously rejecting paths of "scholastic learning." They would not study and become rabbis. The very fact of them gave a degree of stature and significance to the craftsman working with his hands that Hicks the coach and sign painter had become—thanks mostly to Isaac's decision to keep his younger son from any professional education and indenture him to the Tomilsons.

Hicks's rants against scholastic learning could be cartoonishly extreme, but his opposition wasn't unique to him. Quakerism's need to assert and preserve its special identity within a larger non-Quaker society almost by definition resulted in a defensive rejection of many of the concerns of that wider non-Quaker world—plus the very point of Quakerism is that we receive all we need to know about God through bodily awareness. As Edwin H. Cady described it in his study of John Woolman, "A doctrine of truth inwardly known by mystical practices easily produces anti-intellectualism."

Edward probably wasn't alone among Friends, either, in referring to "our Quaker revolution." Quakerism did present, in its operating makeup, a more democratic model than the Anglican Church or any other Protestant denomination, let alone Catholicism. But Hicks may have been unusual among Friends in blending together in his mind the Quaker revolution—and the "primitive republicanism" of Christ and his followers, as he put it—with the American Revolution. It was an even clearer strike against authoritarianism, and Hicks, as his paintings show, was plainly in love with its heroes. He may have stood out among Friends also for his frank celebration of military prowess—at least when the cause was righteous, as it certainly was, he was sure, in 1776. And it was the American Revolution, of course, that stripped his grandfather Gilbert Hicks of his known world and then probably put him to death, and that for many years ruined Isaac's life.

• • •

AND YET THE HICKS FAMILY had a hold on Edward, in direct and indirect ways, all through his life. Among his foremost possessions were letters from his mother to his father. According to Alice Ford, he is thought to have kept them "on his person and read and re-read them," and Eleanore Price Mather wrote that they were in his pocket when he died. They were probably written in the early 1770s, when Catherine and Isaac were first married, or before Edward was born. They have been called love letters, and although they were not written precisely as such, Catherine does call Isaac "my Life," and at one point she writes, "I exist only in your Dear Company. I never knew till now how Essential you were to my Happiness. You, my Soul, know how well I love you . . . I long to see you and lie in your Dear Arms. I miss you much in the Day but a Vast Deal more at Night."

For someone who essentially did not know his mother and grew up in a world with few traces of her (and who wanted to believe that she had been visited by a Quaker-like faith at her death), these letters, with her voice intact, were the next best thing to being with her. Yet while the letters were Catherine's, they were almost as much about Isaac, and finding that Isaac elicited such warmth from his wife makes a follower of Edward's story see his father in a different light.

To the Isaac who gave up his youngest child to the Twinings, and later had him indentured in a manual trade—and who was known in Newtown for years as Squire Hicks, the crusty, even forbidding judge—the letters give us a husband who was, Catherine makes us feel, a loving and embraceable young man. And while the older Isaac was not a convivial figure, he remained in touch with larger issues. Always a voluminous reader, he gave to Newtown the land, which was next to where he lived, for the building of the town library. (Its sign, made by Edward—for $1—and extant, shows Benjamin Franklin reading.) In honor of his gift, Isaac was given a lifetime pass for checking out books in what was the foremost library in the county. This was a much-appreciated gesture since Isaac, then in his late seventies, was putting his years of reading to use in writing a book called *Chronology of the Great Events, from the Creation to A. D. 1825.*

Isaac was, further, the author of some of the most striking words in Ford's biography of Edward. The time was 1791, when Isaac, unable to bring up his three children himself—and struggling after the Revolution, in an adverse political climate, to reassert himself as a judge—sent a letter to a local official seeking help. In the course of describing his reduced situation, he wrote "I have once been somebody but now am hardly anybody." With any assistance, he continued, "I could be once more made a little somebody." Isaac's phrases hold us with their ageless lyrical clarity—and with their relevance to Edward.

Isaac, of course, was talking about the need for a job. He was not puffing himself up. But his few words put in place an attitude that filled Edward, whether because of who he was by temperament or because of the circumstances of his upbringing, or both, with hostility. It is what made him see a haven in the Society of Friends. In the Quakers he joined a world that saw selflessness, or a quest not to stand out, as the only way to achieve union with Christ, or peace. Yet much as he was enamored of and fiercely defended the idea, Edward remained bedeviled by what he saw as the eruptions of his vanity and ego—or, really, by a need to be a somebody. Fortunately for us, he could never resolve the conflict. If he had, there would have been no Kingdoms.

• • •

HICKS'S *MEMOIRS OF THE LIFE* has been treated in a gingerly fashion by some commentators on the artist. It has been noted that his autobiography is an example of a type of Quaker writing. Quakers often kept journals, and the expectation was that they would be published. After the Bible, they were the books that they were likeliest to read, and the journals tended to follow a pattern: the mistakes and waywardness of youth were laid bare, followed by the author's coming to a deeper awareness through Christ. The writings of ministers were particularly valuable because they brought accounts of travel to far-flung meetings. These narrative strands are, a bit tenuously, what Hicks gives us.

Unlike many Quaker ministers, he didn't keep a regular, ongoing journal. It was only on April 4th, 1843, his sixty-third birthday, that Hicks began his memoirs, a slightly different order of writing. After working on it for about a year, he believed he had said everything that was needed. Then in 1846, finding that he had not exhausted the subject, he began a "little diary," which he continued for a bit over a year (and then returned to very briefly just before he died). It is about the same considerable length as the memoirs. The two parts, along with two sermons, make up the volume that was brought out in 1851, not long after his death, as *Memoirs of the Life and Religious Labors of Edward Hicks*.

The book as published has been considered a softened version of Hicks's original manuscript. Carolyn Weekley noted that names were removed from the text he left and that his writer's voice was modulated by people who probably thought they were representing his best interests. Alice Ford, on the other hand, states definitively that "the book is virtually identical with the original, written in longhand by Edward." Whatever adulterations it may have sustained, and typical of other Quaker writing as it might be, the published version is not, however, an anemic affair. It remains available in a reprint of its 1851 self, and just looking at the layout of the pages, with their compressed, boxy units of text, makes it seem as if we have entered Hicks's world.

As a memoirist and diarist, Hicks is, of course, highly repetitious. How could the painter of sixty-odd *Peaceable Kingdom*s not be repetitious? And it goes without saying that if we don't bring to the book a love for Hicks the artist—or have a limited ability to read pronouncements of Christian faith or aren't historically-minded Quakers—we can get lost in the arguments and the details. Yet Hicks was not quite like anyone, whether as a person, a Quaker, or an artist, and my own experience with other Quaker journals, limited to John Woolman's celebrated *Journal*—with its moments of tense awareness about fraught situations—and excerpts from others, gives me the sense that few of them have the flow of peppery opinions, the cascades of disapprobation, or the flights of language that mark Hicks's writing.

Whatever bowdlerization went on with his manuscript, Hicks's feelings for people, religion, and language keep breaking through, as when we hear that the meeting at East Caln has been "scattered, shattered, and peeled" by the controversies of the day. When, in another instance, we encounter Edward's comments about "a J. M., who has been trying nearly twenty years, to convince his friends that he was a great preacher," and then read that "his companion in speechification, W. L., I do not consider worthy of notice," we find this duo of second-rateness oddly real. We almost wish we could hear for a moment their not very good preaching. (With some wit, Mather said about Hicks's comments on his fellows only that they were "crisp.") As an extended piece of writing by an American painter, *Memoirs of the Life* ranks high—though it is not in the same league as George Catlin's *North American Indians*, the now generally used title of his vivid 1841 account of his travels to paint Native American tribes.

Reading Hicks, we are struck by how enjoyable his combativeness can be. Just as, with the animals in the Kingdoms, it is the killers—the carnivores—we are most attracted to, in his writing it is when he lets loose his invective on his villains, or talks about his own various villainies, that his words are most alive. (This of course is often the case with writers of memoirs, of whatever era.) Edward became a carouser while working for the Tomilsons. "I was a swearer and a liar," he says; and, "exceedingly fond" of singing and dancing (and girls), he at one point sang "all the way home" from Philadelphia—in a snowstorm—"besides stopping at several taverns to drink."

Reaching his early twenties, he found himself weeping and distraught when not carrying on. His childhood immersion in the Bible can be heard when he says of this time: "But in the midst of all this sanguine cheer, and streamers gay, when I had cut my cable and launched into the world, my SAVIOUR did not forsake me, for I was not a reprobate, therefore he was still *in* me, and had only retired as it were to the hinder part of my little ship, and was apparently asleep."

At twenty-three, in 1803, he wed his first love, Sarah Worstall, who was a Quaker (as was the senior Gilbert Hicks's wife, Edward's grandmother). Thinking that there might be an anchor for him in religion, he looked to the Society of Friends for an answer. (He was trying out the Methodists at the same time.) He must have felt at home in the realm of Quaker quietism at its most disapproving. A practiced hand in noting his own faults, he announced that he "got to be a great talker, and a great fault finder." This prompts one of his more obnoxious, and charming, confessions: "I was moreover a very zealous temperance man, and of course denounced every one, particularly Friends." A distant relation of Sarah's so irks him (because of the man's deist thinking) that Hicks imagines whipping him until blood runs "down to his heels"—and adds "Thus I went staggering along."

It was seven years until, in 1810, at age thirty, he finally could speak at a meeting for worship, and the occasion and its afterglow were momentous: "For two or three weeks," he writes, "I loved every one I saw." But the Society and eventually life as a minister, which began in 1813, provided new fields of cant and the formulaic to lash out against. With his nose for phoniness, he could make distinctions among the poseurs, as when he grudgingly says, "This man appeared to be one of the better sort of hypocrites."

Praise made him suspicious. Vain as he proclaims himself, he can see, in a typical instance, that "my sermon was of such a character that I have reason to fear it was either an *old one,* or a *borrowed one,* for the Methodist minister asked me for a copy of it as soon as meeting broke up." He shrewdly notes that "even Quaker preachers" can get addicted to preaching, and their listeners can become habituated to their manner, "till the whole concern terminates in a lifeless form."

Rife with manias himself, he saw Quakers having the same problem. "I have noticed that when Friends give way to unsettlement, they hardly know when to stop." He was certainly opposed to slavery; especially in his early years, temperance and abolitionism were his chief obsessions. But he felt later on that abolitionism in Quaker communities had taken on a disruptive life of its own, leading him to distinguish between the "*sober, serious testimony* against Slavery, recognized by the Society of Friends" and the "present *abolition mania*" of Quakers. The fervor, he is certain, leads to "lawyers and lecturers" invading meetinghouses, with other manias—phrenology, for one—not far behind; and then, he goes on, "To cap the climax of absurdity, and show what ridiculous inconsistency Friends are running into," they "profess to believe in a system of deception called animal magnetism."

Hicks's inability to refrain from blurting out the truth as he saw it—he calls himself at one point "constitutionally choleric, turbulent, and haughty"—leads to his having "enemies." When his approach is questioned in a letter that he has received, he lets loose a peerlessly haughty and Biblically-cadenced response: "I would not go over the sill of my door to clear up a report that is nothing but an effervescence of the gall of bitterness in the bond of iniquity." A constant target is anyone paid to officiate at any religious observance. Taking off from John Milton's "hireling ministers," Hicks adds dread to the image by referring to the "prowling hireling." He notes a young man, brought up to be a carpenter, a high station indeed for Hicks, "whom the priests and their satellites persuaded to go to some eastern college to study idleness, arrogance, and speculation, preparatory, perhaps, for holy orders." (Studying idleness is excellent.) Almost as good as "prowling hireling" is "gentlemen dentists," by which he somehow means, or seems to cover, the entire medical profession.

Doctors, whose chief crime seems to be that they charged too much, always stirred his wrath. He amusingly conjures up a deathbed scene "when the sun, the moon, the stars, and every constellation of heaven, is sinking into everlasting obscurity—yea, the very heavens themselves seem rolling together as a scroll, and eternity presenting to our view"—

and, naturally, at this moment, we are by definition "surrounded by a set of consulting Doctors." It is a toss-up whether his greatest scorn is reserved for priests of any denomination, doctors of any variety, lawyers, or creditors, whom he calls usurers. A medieval person in some respect, Edward firmly believed that when you borrow money, as he needed to, interest on a loan is the devil's work.

• • •

GIVEN HICKS'S BARBED, RESTLESS, and paranoid temperament, and his particular set of prejudices—and his ideals—the conflict that erupted among Quakers in the early decades of the nineteenth century can seem like something he created. The rift in the Society, which was a kind of playing out again, as Edward practically described it, of the American Revolution, was real and painful. It gathered steam beginning in the late 1810s and came to a head in 1827 and 1828—and was only resolved, at least formally, in 1955. It has been said that the tear never healed over.

The Society had of course been changing since its turbulent early years under George Fox. The rise in the following century of quietism stamped Quakers with a clearer identity for themselves and within all of the population, but it had a hampering, exclusionary tone. The Quaker historian Bliss Forbush wrote that it was "unsuited for great spiritual adventure or missionary conquest," and whether or not this is accurate, the quietist spirit did not appeal to all Friends.

In principle, working in trade or merchandizing was not frowned upon by Quakers. Quite the contrary. And by the early nineteenth century, Friends in urban areas, especially in Philadelphia and New York, were living differently from Quakers in rural communities, where farming and the "path of humble industry" kept their incomes far lower than those of their city brethren. Friends in cities didn't have, either, quite the same allegiance to quietist plainness and severity in clothing or in the look of their homes. This split didn't come about overnight. Already in 1756 John Woolman noticed about his fellow Quakers that "many, I fear, are too clogged with the Things of this Life." Later, he recorded at length a minister who saw "marks of outward wealth" among Friends leading to a "Barrenness" of spirit, and in England in the early 1770s

Woolman caught "superfluities" of one kind or another now being "common amongst us."

But Friends in Hicks's day were increasingly receptive as well to thinking that had been coloring Protestant worship in general for some time. This was evangelical Christianity, a zealous, muscular, converting, revivalist Protestantism that put a premium on the literal truth of the Bible. Quakers themselves had been evangelical in spirit in the 1600s, when the faith was starting out. Early Quakers wanted very much to spread their word and make more people Friends. But the evangelical Protestantism that started gaining traction in the later eighteenth century had a different emphasis. It tended to see people as inherently sinful and damned but capable of saving themselves through a new allegiance to Christ.

Many urban Friends, particularly elders in Philadelphia, the center of American Quakerism, and to a lesser extent in New York and Baltimore, were drawn to the more defined and regularized—and controllable—worship that fundamentalism brought with it. It spawned Bible societies and an atmosphere where one confessed one's faith. Much of the friction between Friends centered on Elias Hicks, whose ministry, with its quietist emphasis on the Inner Light, increasingly struck the Orthodox, as Friends veering toward evangelical attitudes were now called, as wrongheaded, even blasphemous.

Tall and imposing in appearance, Elias had a magnetic personality though he was not a firebrand. He was Edward's second cousin, and, born in 1748, a generation or so older. He and Edward corresponded and were in general agreement about the growing discord. An 1825 publication brought together sermons that the two of them gave in New York, and they were together at meetings on Long Island and elsewhere. Elias was a good friend of Walt Whitman's grandfather, and Whitman—who was, like Emerson, much attracted to Quaker thinking—kept a death mask of Elias in his Camden home. In his later years, Whitman wrote about the minister with real warmth.

We certainly feel Elias's stature in his vigorous and long-standing concern with slavery, one facet of which was his proposal to boycott any products, including cotton, rice, and sugar, made with such labor. He wasn't, as the earlier writings of John Woolman in particular bear out, the first Quaker to urge this plan be followed, but little had come of it in Woolman's day or after. Elias's powerful tract, written in 1810—it was published some two decades before abolition began to take shape as a movement in the North—at the least made a different generation of Friends aware of the terror and criminality of the slave system that was very much in existence in half of the country. His fierce belief that there was no difference between owning a slave and buying the "fruits of slave labor" seemed to rile Quakers of every persuasion.

In his travels, along with attending countless meetings, Elias addressed Baptists—he preached to them to desist from baptizing!—and Methodists (and no doubt less clear-cut denominations). He logged in many thousands of miles in his ministerial journeys over the years, and his appeal and his fame were such that in one case, with so many people wanting to hear him, the governor of New Jersey gave him the state house in Trenton for the event, and he spoke twice in state buildings in Albany. Whitman remembered being taken, at age ten, by his parents to hear Elias speak in the ballroom of a hotel in Brooklyn Heights—an "opulent and worldly setting," wrote Justin Kaplan, where the audience included, "along with working-class people like the Whitmans . . . the city's dignitaries and social leaders, merchants and judges, men and women of fashion, naval officers in uniform, and elderly Quakers in broad-brimmed hats and black bonnets."

Whitman said that Elias, onstage, could be dramatically vehement one moment and earnest and eloquent the next. Elias's writings convey chiefly his gravity, though sometimes his phrases hold you, either because they propose an idea you might debate with yourself—as when he says "The business of life is to turn inward"—or because his choice of words is in itself stimulating. When Elias writes "Our hearts are filled with many guests—many beloveds," the thought of our having guests within us can make us want to stop reading and think of how true the metaphor might be. Immediately vivid and comprehensible, too, is his saying about God that "He has from my childhood showed me the way faster than I was willing to walk in it." "Business," "guests," "faster"—each plain word lights up its sentence.

Writing in his journal about how ministers ought to prepare for giving sermons, Elias essentially said: do not prepare. He urged them instead "carefully to wait in the nothingness and emptiness of self, that what they speak may be only what the Holy Spirit speaketh to them." The "nothingness and emptiness of self" is a distinctly quietist idea; quietist Quakers believed in a kind of emptying out of all one's emotions, much the way they favored the plain and unadorned in their homes and appearance. Whatever its lineage, there remains an undeniable potency to the image that the words bring forth.

• • •

IT WAS BECAUSE of words that Elias made some of his fellow Quakers nervous, frightened, and hostile. Just as the Bible was becoming newly sacrosanct, much of his preaching asked for Friends and his listeners of other faiths not to ride on every word of the Scriptures. Anthony Benezet had already put a dent in the idea that the Bible had to be taken as literal truth, but Elias went further. He saw the Bible as a storehouse of metaphors, some more alive and pertinent than others, and not as a work of history—and certainly not as a fund for the creation of creeds and doctrines.

He truly believed that the business of life is to turn inward and that you get there entirely by yourself. That was what the silent meeting for worship was about. Elias followed through on this Quaker creation logically, saying that it isn't necessary to know how to read or write to perceive the Inner Light. Further, he believed the creeds of this or that Protestant church to be no more than opinions. He was profoundly opposed to the way evangelicals sought a uniformity of belief. He could say, and believe, for example, that Confucianism was hardly less inspired than the Old and New Testaments—not a winning idea in the larger English-speaking world of the time, where a dogmatic Christianity had an increasingly wide popular appeal.

In the reasonableness and sense of freedom inhering in Elias's thought, he can feel like a secular, modern person. His thinking makes understandable why Emerson, seeking an intensification of consciousness in a somewhat different way, could have felt, as F. O. Matthiessen wrote, "more kinship with the inner light of the Quakers than with any formal creed." (Traveling as a lecturer first in New England and then throughout many states, beginning in the 1830s, Emerson was something of a confrere of the stereotypical intrepid Quaker minister.)

Elias and his point of view were in fact labeled "liberal." The terms of this fraught time in the 1820s can be confusing, however, when we also connect Elias with his quietist beliefs. He was opposed to developments at the time which we would think progressive, such as the creation of canals and railroad lines, which are about linking people and shrinking the space that separates them. New forms of transportation worked to dispel the isolated, unconnected life that Elias believed Quakers needed. Worldliness seemed ungodly to him, and he objected when his daughters were drawn to the new (non-drab) fashions.

By the same token, it is odd to think of Quakers living in cities and thriving in a monied milieu as being receptive to evangelical dictates and pieties. The situation seems topsy-turvy. It was rural, and less well-to-do, Friends—and determinedly uncosmopolitan Friends—who represented the more flexible and unconventional, almost the more worldly, view of a religious life.

Given his susceptibility for conflict, Edward saw the Quaker rift in stark, charged terms. He called the two sides, in his *Memoirs*, merely Friends and Orthodox, and a reader finds little or nothing in the book about the themes or issues at stake, or what each side wanted. Without setting any stages, Edward takes us right into the effrontery of the Orthodox and the rancor of the moment. It is the tempers, the textures, and the color of the war that excited him. His reactions were personal and physical. The Orthodox were "coldly pursuing a malignant, unjust plan of operations, that has for its object, all the injury they could possibly inflict." He adds, "I confess I never had any thing so to try me as the *cold*, supercilious and insulting manner in which they entered our houses."

The move to give the Society a more evangelical character had begun in England, and many of the ministers carrying the new ideas were English (and a fair number were women). This being the case, Edward's anti-British fervor was inflamed—the embers had never fully gone cold—and he naturally and with serious justification judged the would-be Orthodox putsch as aristocratic and undemocratic in nature. He saw the Orthodox as comprised of "the English and Royal Americans." (Not that the Quakerism that Edward and Elias favored was free from a repressive, even autocratic, way of managing everyday life.) The Society's riven state was noticeable in Britain and even to those who, like Charles Lamb, were not themselves Friends. But Lamb couldn't say whether Quakers "in our days have kept to the primitive spirit, or in what proportion they have substituted formality for it." The answer, he felt, lay with the "Judge of Spirits."

Edward, his own Judge of Spirits, viewed the event, without drawing parallels to his own experience, as a crisis about separation. The Society of Friends, which gave him when he was still a boy a needed sense of a welcoming family, was being rent itself. "The English Friends," Edward wrote with characteristic hyperbole, "spread themselves over the continent, and wherever they went they separated husbands and wives, parents and children, brothers and sisters, and the nearest and dearest friends." He says this in two different places in his memoirs. The incivilities must have felt like a grave embarrassment—a loss of face within American life as a whole—to many Quakers. Hicks felt it was. In a letter to his friend Hugh Balderston, he remembers how, on the trip they made to the "western country," they met someone one day who asked, "Have you Quakers done quarreling yet? I think you ought to be ashamed of yourselves." Edward went on, "Ah, dear Hugh, I think so too." Yet it is unlikely that other Friends, regardless of the faction they were part of, saw the unfolding drama so fully in Edward's primal terms.

Along with Elias and an old friend named John Comly, who had been instrumental in steering the young Edward to Quakerism in the first place—and who helped look out for the painter's welfare throughout his life—Edward was one of the leaders of the so-called Hicksite group. (The label had to do with Elias, not Edward, and, as David Tatham pointed out, it was given by the Orthodox, and meant disparagingly, while the term "Orthodox" was bestowed on them, and also meant to wound, by their country opponents.) Edward describes the developments, heading to showdowns at meetings in Philadelphia in 1827, in military and warlike, and wildly un-Quakerish, terms. "At meeting," he writes about Elias at one point, "his enemies appeared in battle array"—the reader stops, wondering what these folks looked like—and a "drawn battle was fought." We hear about factions gaining "the ascendancy" and "carrying all before them"—and "flushed with victory and confident of success."

If his racing descriptions are any indication of his spirit as he recollected the time, Edward was buoyed by the clash; and the "battle" ended in "victory." Most of the meetings supported Elias and his more mystical, less dogmatic approach, though the Orthodox were hardly trounced, and a formal Separation was declared in 1827. In some meetings the congregants were almost evenly divided. And as Quakerism in time spread through the South and into the West, the more Bible-centered and evangelical approach—including pastors leading the proceedings and hymns being sung—took hold. Further separations and splinterings followed as the century wore on. But when the shooting was over from the first and the most storied schism, Elias could say that the issue of the Society's direction had altogether less substance than the abolition of slavery.

The Kingdoms

In the end, Edward may have been more affected by the animosity and bitterness surrounding the Separation than Elias. Edward felt, in his autobiographical account, that he had been guilty of excessive pride during the skirmishes, and he ended his memoirs with a call for comity. He confessed that in some sense he was little different from his opponents. The Orthodox minister J. Evans, for instance, "was a violent, choleric man, and too much like myself, malignant and bitter against his enemies." But then Hicks was always finding himself in situations that weren't as dire as he first thought, or with people who didn't judge him as severely as he assumed—or were, like his Orthodox foe J. Evans, rather like himself. "Had the company of a friend in the afternoon," he wrote in his diary in one of a number of such moments, "that I was rather glad of, for I had feared that I had offended him when at the funeral of his father."

Hicks's *Peaceable Kingdoms* are in some way about this second act in his thinking: this desire to pull back from his anger and even erase it. The pictures can be seen as confessions of his intemperateness, or exhortations to be a better person—to make amends for his emotional violence, his partisanship, his selfish vanity, his free-floating criticism of others (and of himself). The more clear-cut reason for his creating paintings of the prophesy in Isaiah was, of course, to ask for hostilities in his Quaker world to be relinquished—hostilities stoked to a degree by his own pronouncements as a minister. In this light, the lion, leopard, and other carnivores represent the Orthodox, and the innocent, tame animals are the Liberal or Hicksite wing of the Society.

It has also been said by Eleanore Price Mather, and amplified by Carolyn Weekley, that Hicks chose the subject of the Old Testament prophesy because its message of peaceful coexistence was so in line with Quaker thinking—it was literally a painted poster for the Society—that it gave him a justification and a cover for his desire to make easel pictures. The subject "legitimized" his painting. But surely this cannot mean that he kept recreating the prophesy because it provided him with the only image his fellow Quakers could accept. What legitimized his other kinds of paintings?

Much of the strength of the Kingdoms comes from the way they don't feel tied to distinct allegorical points and at the same time lend themselves to different interpretations. In addition to seeing, in our two sets of beasts, Orthodox and Liberal Quakers, we might be encountering the other family division in Hicks's mind. The carnivores could be the greater Hicks family, with their establishment ways and Tory sympathies—the lion, after all, is an emblem of Britain—while the innocent, domesticated creatures could be Friends, the people who formed Hicks's substitute family. Maybe this is why the ox, over time, became so big in size and so central a figure in the gathering. In the ox the innocent have at least one member with the dramatic (if stilled) presence of the flashier carnivores.

But we don't always automatically note that we look at two radically different kinds of creatures, or that we see wild beasts who have momentarily relinquished their ferocity. Most of the time I think we remind ourselves of these distinctions. We can feel that we are looking at Quakerism itself—that is to say, a Kingdom might represent not the warring parties of the day but a fundamental aspect of the Society: the meeting. Seeing people in set groups made up a large part of Hicks's life. In the raised minister's gallery, where he sat for decades, he would always be looking out toward a congregation, not all of whom were equally alert (or, apparently, especially on winter mornings, awake). But mostly what we take in, I believe, is an ever-shifting group of possibly related and clearly unequal members.

• • •

A KIND OF INDEFINITENESS also played over Hicks's role as a creator. On one public occasion he spoke positively about art, but his words "upset" the congregation, wrote Arthur Edwin Bye, and elicited a visit from a disapproving committee, before whom he needed to defend himself and defuse the situation. But this event, which took place at Makefield meeting, is anomalous. What prevailed instead was a cloudier climate where different Friends tolerated what he did, or simply were unaware of it—or expressed warm thanks if they were given a Kingdom—or would be ready to disapprove again if he made too outright a case for his activity.

It is generally thought that Hicks could keep making his easel pictures, and the elders in question would not needle him over it—and remember, this was a religion where a Friend who attended a non-Quaker wedding could be disowned—because of his value to the community as a minister. It was a matter of strategically intended overlooking (which is funny since the subject is pictures), and something of the same planned avoidance went on in Hicks's mind as he thought about his artworks. He seems to have believed that there was a distinction between art (not good) and painting (acceptable), and that his Kingdoms and farms and so on were the latter—but at no point was the issue drawn out this clearly.

Needless to say, he never participated in an art exhibition, or apparently even went to one; and while his children (and grandchildren) attended exhibitions, Edward could cast aspersions on people who paid to see art. His easel paintings go unmentioned in his densely detailed memoirs and in his equally detailed diary, and they are not listed in his office records, where he (or his son Isaac) listed his every job.

Yet in cousin Thomas's portrait, Edward is shown with his brushes and palette in hand, seated next to an easel on which is one of his Kingdoms. He could hardly appear to be more of an artist. But maybe he thought he was coming across as that safer entity, a "painter." In the introduction to his memoirs, he writes that his "nature" had kept him from being an "exemplary" Friend, one factor being his "excessive fondness for painting." He follows the word "painting" with "a trade to which I was brought up, being connected to coach making."

He goes on to call himself periodically a "painter," and almost every time a reader thinks, Oh, here he is forgetting that he wants to present himself only as a craftsman-painter and is talking as the creator that he also was. Referring to a trip he made in a ministerial role that got him as far as Canada, he says he has told some of the anecdotes connected with the journey "so often that perhaps, being a painter, I may have added to them a little fresh color at times." In another moment, where his language reminds us that he was esteemed as a preacher (and corroborating the Shakespearian character of some of his lions), he thinks of death, and is altogether bleak about himself—and concludes this diary entry: "I am nothing but a poor old worthless insignificant painter."

Yet in the few times in his memoirs when he speaks openly of art, he makes it very clear that there is no "fondness" there for him. He calls it "fine" painting, and with denunciatory (and possibly guilt-fueled) words that probably few of his fellow Quakers would have thought necessary for the job, he writes of painting that "it appears clearly to me to be one of those trifling, insignificant arts, which has never been of any substantial advantage to mankind." It is "the inseparable companion of voluptuousness and pride," and is "now enrolled among the premonitory symptoms of the rapid decline of the American Republic." With this blast, he may have felt that, for the record, he had absolved himself of any taint of art.

As might be expected, our knowledge of what weight his easel paintings had at the time is spotty. Alice Ford says that they were "popular," but she doesn't flesh out the statement. Edward's affluent New York City relatives Isaac and Samuel, who helped him financially when his debts mounted, received pictures in thanks, and on at least three occasions Kingdoms were commissioned. Edward wrote in 1838 to Samuel Hart, who was, like Edward's father, a Bucks County land surveyor and justice of the peace—and a recipient of a Kingdom—that some of the pictures were made in order to "raise money to bear my expenses" from a recent trip as a minister. Hicks's casting them as merely possible sources of money accords with the way he kept his easel paintings at arm's length in general.

In an 1836 letter that he addressed to a Luis Jones (whose name was probably Louis), Hicks spoke openly and realistically about selling them. He sounds like any artist of any period—i.e., quick to be ambivalent about what he was doing—when he wrote, "I have been uneasy about giving thee the trouble of selling my paintings. I have been very much discouraged about them and indeed everything else." He goes on, "If I can get rid of them at almost any rate, I think I will never paint any more"—and concludes, "thee may sell them for anything or nothing, or give them away, or burn them; don't give thyself any more trouble."

The early history of about a quarter of the Kingdoms is unknown, meaning that these pictures might have been sold. The majority, however, were given as gifts to immediate and greater family members. They went as well to friends as tokens of Edward's affection and appreciation —to doctors that the Hickses saw over the years, lawyer friends, a fellow minister. His paintings of other subjects, too, went largely as gifts, though again the fair number of examples whose original provenance is unknown might have been sold. A version of Washington at the Delaware was apparently used as payment for a Newtown dental bill.

• • •

DETERMINED TO DISTANCE HIMSELF from "fine" painting, Hicks might point to the fact that the majority of his canvases derived from pictures that he found in different publications. He could say to any Quaker elder or minister, or to his conscience, that artistic creativity was nothing he was guilty of because he was merely a conduit for existing images. He got underway as an artist by using a contemporary engraving, found in a Bible, of the prophesy of Isaiah by Richard Westall. This Englishman may be best known for giving Hicks his impetus and for being at one point the young Queen Victoria's drawing instructor. In later years, adding figures to the scene that are part of Isaiah's verses but are not found in Westall's illustration, Hicks used other images that he saw in Bibles (they were generally illustrated at the time) or in various gazettes.

His historical paintings, however, show him taking few liberties with his sources. The picture of Penn and his treaty came from an engraving of 1775 by John Hull of a painting of the subject by Benjamin West. Hicks's image of the signing of the Declaration of Independence derived from a print of John Trumbull's painting of the moment, and a print of the original canvas was undoubtedly the source for his version of Sully's *The Passage of the Delaware*—a work that was also copied by other artists, including the lively primitive painter George Washington Mark. Hicks's paintings of Niagara Falls came from a self-contained scene that was at the bottom of a map by Henry S. Tanner, published in 1822, of North

America; and the 1846 *Noah's Ark* was based closely on a lithograph that had been published by Nathaniel Currier two years earlier.

The only compositions that were largely his alone were the farm scenes that he made in his last years. But even here we find that the cattle at the bottoms of the scenes came from agricultural publications—and, rather wittily, in his paintings of David Twining's home and farm, a fellow in a long coat getting onto a horse comes from Sully's painting of Washington at the Delaware. I confess that when I learned the full extent of Hicks's borrowings, I was a little nonplussed. Even some particularly lovable details, such as the way, in the early Kingdoms, the wolf and the leopard are seen on their bellies, their heads on forepaws that are placed neatly before them, are in Westall's print. It was Westall who, charmingly, made the wolf resemble dogs who get into a restful position yet still want to keep the people in the room in sight.

Although Hicks the borrower is a topic that has been acknowledged, most commentators don't seem to think it is a large issue. But it can be bothersome. Julius Held, whose point was to chip away at a reputation he saw as inflated, offered as his crowning blow that since Hicks copied his images, he "freed . . . his artistic activity from the struggles and triumphs which a real creative effort entails." (Where such a pronouncement leaves musicians and actors, who generally don't write the music they perform or the lines they speak, is left unsaid.) Alice Ford, though enough of an admirer of Hicks to write two books about him, felt that he was in some ways in the class of Henri Rousseau—except that the American was "primarily a copyist. He did not permit his creative imagination the unbridled and exotic range which marks the works of Rousseau." Hicks the artist ultimately was bound, she believed—and I think Mather and Weekley, his other principal commentators, believe—to Quaker precepts.

Since the days, however, of the Post-Impressionists, and then the Fauves and the Cubists, art has been many things in addition to a realistically painted or drawn record of the world we see, and our notions of art and of originality have tremendously expanded. Artworks have become increasingly about the artist's thinking and intentions—or about what earlier twentieth-century generations, excited primarily by issues of form, would call merely the literary, storytelling, or biographical aspects of art. In this climate the idea that a body of work could be a rethinking of already existing images seems more adventurous than specious. If Hicks were an artist of the past few decades he might make the fact that his work consisted primarily of reworkings of the same image done over time his very point. His many *Peaceable Kingdoms* could be seen (and accepted) as evidence of a thirty-year-long piece of performance art.

Sheer copying, though, doesn't exactly describe Hicks's method with the Kingdoms. From the beginning he tinkered with his sources, enlarging or cropping them, or making images that bring together elements from different sources. Hicks's shepherding into one scene creatures from different places made his Kingdoms, in effect—as Ford noticed—collages. His approach accounts for one of the most appealing aspects of these paintings: the way his animals and his little accompanying children, whether standing, lounging, or curled into themselves, bob a little, like boats or balloons moored for the moment. Each, after all, is an insert from somewhere.

Perhaps Léger's enthusiasm when he saw a Kingdom on that early trip to New York came from his noting a brother in arms. The French painter's figures are also large-scale forms that look as if they are momentarily held in place and, if dislodged, could float off. More than that, Hicks may have actually influenced Léger. In his well-known *Leisure* (1944–49), begun on a later stay in the States, Léger alludes to the French classicist tradition he was a part of with an inscription, "Homage à Louis David," on a piece of paper in the scene. It has been said that he might as easily have referred to Henri Rousseau, whose paintings of the outings of the French middle class are echoed in *Leisure*.

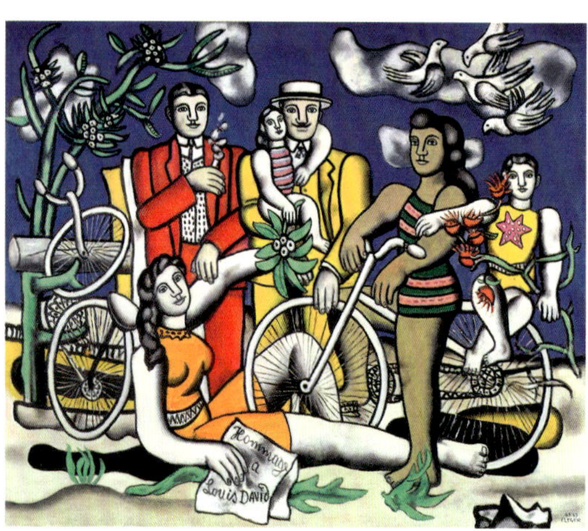

Fernand Léger, *Leisure: Hommage à Louis David*, 1948–49, 60 1/2 × 72 3/4 in. (154 × 185 cm).

But the entire arrangement of grown-ups and children in the painting, with its seeming casualness, recalls Hicks as well—and isn't the young woman stretched out at the bottom the descendant of the many elongated leopards that hold down the lower part of numerous Kingdoms? When I told the painter Dona Nelson that I was writing on Hicks, she said she "always considered him early Pop." At first this surprised me, yet it makes sense when Hicks's cousinship with Léger is thought about, because the French painter, in his quest to make art about public experience, set forth in large, projecting forms, was surely "early Pop" himself.

• • •

THE EARLIEST IN DATE of the *Peaceable Kingdoms* is a revelation and a treat. In the Kingdom dated 1816–18, in the Cleveland Museum, we are seeing Hicks's idea in embryo. It shows how from an early (if not the earliest) moment he was both very careful in copying his Westall print source and could disregard it entirely.

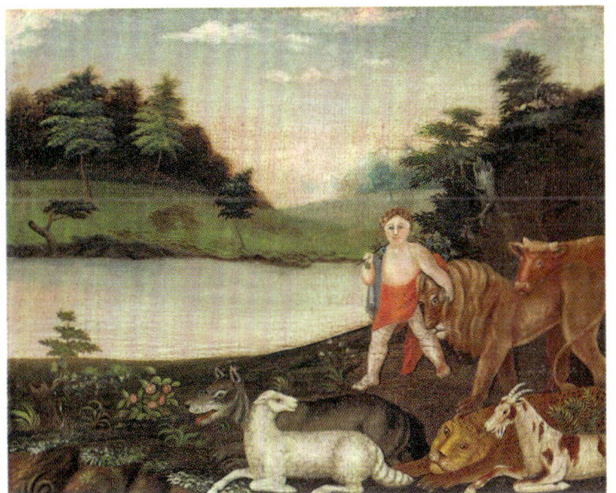

Edward Hicks, *Peaceable Kingdom*, c. 1816–18, 18 3/4 × 23 1/2 in. (47.6 × 59.7 cm).

He wanted to get the child, whose identity in Isaiah's passage is unclear, planted in precisely the assertive, leg's-spread way Westall had it. Hicks also liked the way the boy stands with one arm touching the little lion, who nuzzles up to him. In the many Kingdoms to come the child's appearance will change radically. The child, though, will almost always have an arm out to touch one of the creatures.

Yet in most of this first Kingdom, Hicks was on his own. Where Westall set his illustration in a wooded nowhere, Hicks already had a full structure in mind: he knew that he wanted the prophesy to take up mostly the right side of a larger landscape, which would include a body of water—and water that would give off light. This is a crucial alteration to the little source.

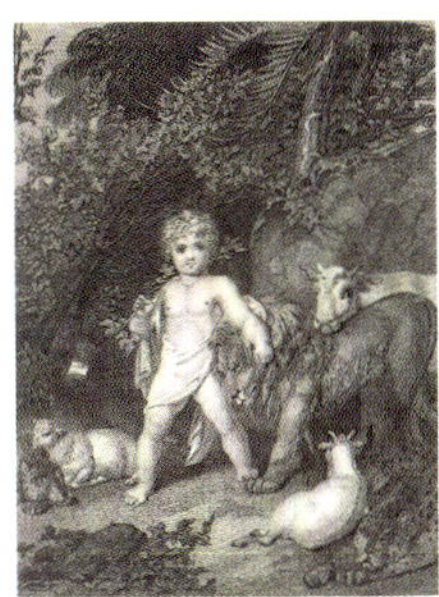

Engraving after Richard Westall drawing, *The Peaceable Kingdom of the Branch*, 1800–15.

Hicks was also already concerned with eyes. Westall's leopard and lion have their eyes closed or nearly closed, perhaps to indicate their newly pacified nature. Hicks improves this. Subtly and masterfully, with no more than showing the lion with a fully open eye and changing the line of his mouth, Hicks gives the animal the first of the many character parts he will play. This is a brooding, or possibly perturbed, or maybe just preoccupied, lion. The leopard, who now looks out at us, also has the rudiments of the demeanor—watchful, noncommittal, languorous—he will have in future paintings.

Hicks would never again give the kid, the lamb, or the wolf the prominence he gives them in Cleveland's painting. Yet the mysterious hiddenness of the wolf—his character throughout the Kingdoms—is already partially in place. Where Hicks has opened the leopard's eyes so he can look right at the viewer, and opened fully the lion's eyes so he can, it seems, look inward, he has transformed the wolf's line of sight so we see a creature who makes no contact with anything.

• • •

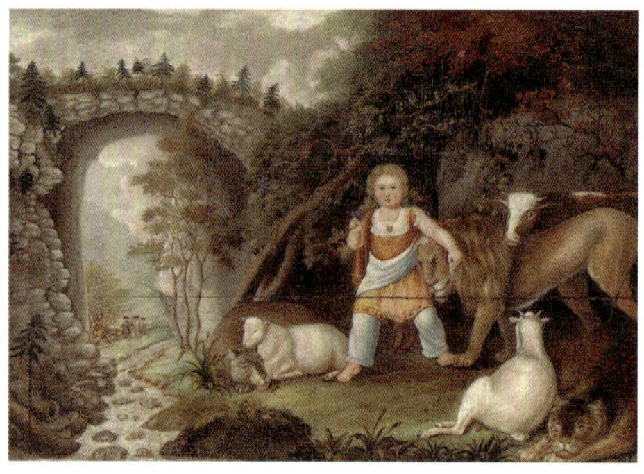

Edward Hicks, *The Peaceable Kingdom of the Branch*, c. 1825–30, 36 1/4 × 44 7/8 in. (92.1 × 114 cm).

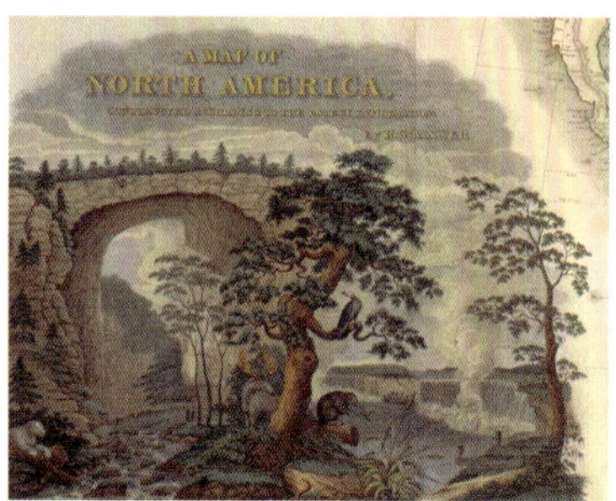

Henry Schenck Tanner, *A Map of North America*, 1822, detail.

When Hicks came back to the *Peaceable Kingdom* a few years after his first version, the conflict between Orthodox Friends and their quietist, or Hicksite, opponents had significantly increased. Maybe this strife accounts for his paying more respectful attention to his Westall source and, at the same time, his going forward with a new degree of purpose and artistic assurance. Hicks returned the carnivores and their innocent mates to precisely the poses Westall had given them (making the liberties he took with the Cleveland picture all the more remarkable). Instead of the lively, introspective, and ambiguous creatures of his first Kingdom we are back to Westall's sleepy pets.

But then Hicks boldly and attractively filled out the landscape on the other side of the group. Working from that vignette on Tanner's map, he added the arching Natural Bridge of Virginia—a phenomenon of nature—and he put under the bridge the scene of Penn making his treaty with the Lenape. This tiny group came from the print of West's painting of the subject. The newly restructured Kingdom thus shows Hicks adroitly blending, at a very early stage in the history of the Kingdoms, images from three disparate sources; and, although the pictures don't have the dry and esoteric quality of symbol-laden works, we can see, in what might be called a visual pun, that there is a "bridge"—a connection—between Penn making his treaty and the disarmament underway among the animals.

Done mostly around 1826, this new way of handling the theme is called the "Peaceable Kingdom of the Branch" because the child holds a branch from a grape vine behind him. The numerous versions of this new approach are also referred to as the "border Kingdoms" because the paintings are set in elaborate frames on which Hicks presented Isaiah's prophesy. Standing before the pictures, you start to read from the left going upward—many of these lines begin "The wolf. . . ." You continue reading along the top, come down on the right, and end with the lines across the bottom.

A sometime versifier, Hicks sometimes put Isaiah's message in his own couplets. Doing so sounds like an example of the industrious naïf exhibiting another talent, but David Tatham perceived that for Orthodox Quakers, Hicks's playing with the Scriptural wording was a provocation. When we read on some pictures: "The wolf also shall dwell with the lamb," the words are the Bible's. When we read on others: "The Wolf shall with the lambkin dwell in peace," the words are Hicks's. The changeover would have been of the same disturbing, even sacrilegious, nature to the evangelically minded as Elias Hicks's saying that the Bible gives us metaphors, not literal truth. Edward was making Elias's thoughts as clear as day. He may have gone beyond Elias's liberal views when in some of the frames he both rewrote Isaiah and gave equal footing to his own:

When the great PENN his famous treaty made
With indian chiefs beneath the elm tree's shade

But probably not that many of the Orthodox saw the pictures.

• • •

THE KINGDOMS OF THE BRANCH are an acquired taste. For most viewers, especially those who are familiar with the stereotypical Kingdom with its commanding lion and sprawling leopard, there is undoubtedly something artificial and decorous about the pictures. Where the best-known Kingdoms are painted with strong, warm oranges, reds, and greens, and have an autumnal softness, the branch or border pictures often leave the impression of a summertime midday stillness, with much greenery and white or pale skies. Most significantly, the animals take a back seat to the child. He, not the lion or the leopard, is the protagonist, and, one of the innocents himself, he is less lovable to us than the beasts.

Yet when these paintings are seen in relation to the Kingdoms in general, they are absorbing. They show a Hicks who in a relatively short time became fully confident about his theme, perhaps because the tensions building among Quakers in 1826 gave him a ready audience for the subject of peace. From the small picture in Cleveland he jumped in size to works that are regularly almost three feet wide. One example, used as a fireboard (a panel that covered a fireplace during warm months), is some four feet wide. His elaborate frames add to the sense of substantiality; the pictures can seem almost massive even when seen in reproduction. The lettering in gold with black shadows, set against backgrounds in alluring and unusual shades of brown or green, caps the luxuriant effect.

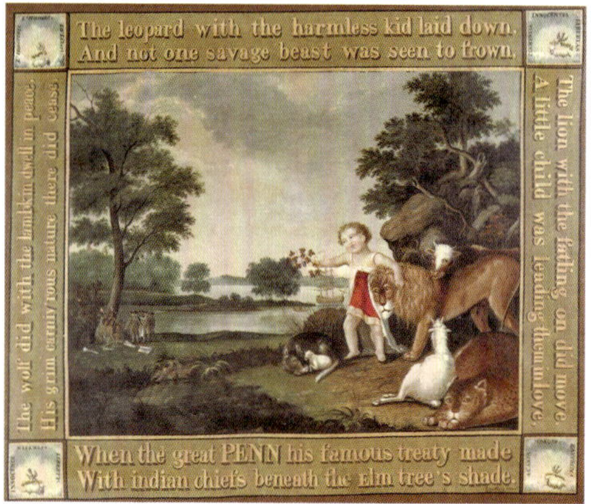

Edward Hicks, *Peaceable Kingdom*, c. 1826, 29 × 36 in. (73.6 × 91.4 cm).

Exposure to a number of the border Kingdoms—more importantly—can make a viewer admire these paintings (or at least want to see more of them) for the very reason that makes them at first a little alienating: their note of decorativeness and artificiality. We know we are looking at pictures that are about sectarian hostilities and a Biblical prophecy; yet in visual, artistic, and dramatic terms these pictures are about order and balance. They give us a Hicks who, coming at it from his own angle, might have been working in the foremost artistic idiom of the day. This was Neoclassicism, a style that reigned in European painting, architecture, and sculpture (and in fashion and interior decoration) from the latter decades of the eighteenth century and came to the fore in America after the Revolution. It suffused American political oratory for years.

Representing almost an infatuation with the perceived spirit and values of, initially, the Roman classical past and subsequently (and more lastingly and significantly) the Greek classical past, Neoclassicism pro ceeded to hold sway in the young republic during the first decades of the nineteenth century. It famously reached one ripened expression in Thomas Jefferson's architecture. With his animus against the fine arts, Hicks, of course, would hardly have set out to make pictures in this spirit, but something of its influence and glamour clearly rubbed off on him.

It is important to note that, like a number of nineteenth-century American painters of the greatest distinction—among them Raphaelle Peale, Thomas Eakins, Mary Cassatt, and John F. Peto—Hicks was a Philadelphia artist in some respects. (When his name is joined to these others, and when Alexander Wilson, whose exquisite drawings of birds remain little known, is added to the list, it makes one feel that in the nineteenth century no other American place contributed as much to the country's art.) Hicks lived nearby, and William Penn's city long held his attention for its role in American Quakerism. It was there that he first spoke at a meeting for worship.

Philadelphia had been, from 1790 to 1800, the nation's (first) capital. In the early nineteenth century, when Hicks was often going there, it was still the country's largest city, and the center of, among many other things, its nascent art world. The city was the site of the country's first art academy and its first art exhibitions. Hicks would make a point of not being concerned with the professional art world, but he had an eagle eye for whatever and whoever posed a threat, and it is hard to believe that in his travels to Philadelphia, especially when he was in his early twenties and still in the process of becoming a Quaker, he missed the city's cosmopolitan culture, which was permeated with Neoclassicism. Besides, this new style and spirit had even touched his home base. As the Bucks County historian Edna S. Pullinger noted (though not in relation to Hicks's pictures), in the early 1820s "there suddenly appeared on the streets of Newtown many rounded doorways, reflecting the growing local interest in Classic architecture."

In the border Kingdoms, for whatever reason, Hicks operated as a kind of classical artist. One feels it in the special clarity of form in these paintings and in their emotional coolness. Their highly important frames bespeak a classical attitude: frames denote limits and structure, and some of these Kingdoms give us frames within frames. The lettering on the frames adds to the pictures' note of formality because, I believe, we less read the lines word for word than take them in as a continuous blocky decorative pattern. But it is the child himself who most conveys, in the tailored contemporary outfits he wears in a few of the pictures, and the way in those pictures he confidently strides forth, the worldly manner of the day.

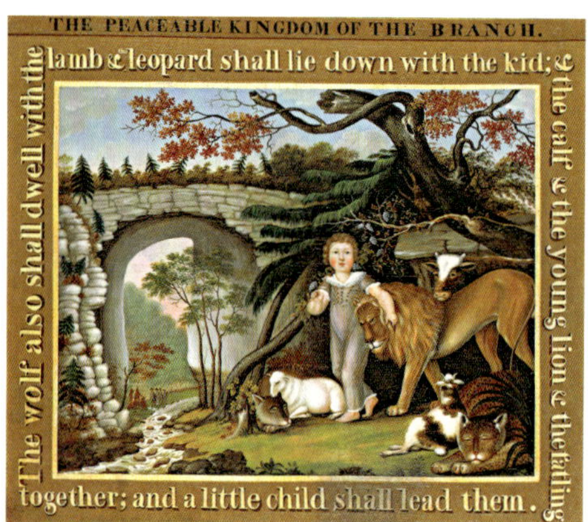

Edward Hicks, *The Peaceable Kingdom of the Branch*, 1822–25, 32 1/4 × 37 3/4 in. (81.9 × 95.9 cm).

• • •

WHO IS THE CHILD? The book of Isaiah was held in high regard by Christians because a number of its verses seemed to foretell a Christian future, and the child, who will "lead" the newly pacified animal family, could be considered a prophet in the making. He could foretell Christ. Richard Westall, in the engraving that set Hicks in motion, may have had this association in mind because he has the boy holding a grapevine over his shoulder. The boy, it is true, sports it in the informal way one might carry a fishing pole, and the sturdy little fellow altogether looks like he mostly has a gym workout on his mind, but Westall's audience would have known that the vine, in Christian interpretation, presages the wine of the Last Supper and Christ's shedding his blood for humanity's sake.

A Quaker would not have subscribed to such symbolism—this is pointed out in Mather and Miller's catalogue—and the evidence clearly supports this. As Hicks evolved his Kingdom over the years, there were stretches where the child almost gets lost in the shuffle and so could hardly represent Christ. If, moreover, he had been a symbol of Christ, the Kingdoms probably could not have been the continuously pliant and changeable pictures that they are. They might instead have been more like the contemporaneous series of paintings by Thomas Cole called *The Voyage of Life,* with their stage-set angels bestowing divine radiance in every scene. Yet to indicate that the child is more than merely a child, he is referred to by some commentators as the Divine Child.

Is it possible that Hicks was initially drawn to the prophesy because the sole humans in it are children? Perhaps because his own childhood, marked as it was with both the disappearance of his parents and the beneficence of Elizabeth Twining, had a stark drama to it, this time in life remained one that Hicks was always close to. His experience taught him that childhood and youth was a time when, as he wrote, the "waste places that your fathers may have thrown down" could be restored. The words come from a significant piece of writing, included in his published memoirs, entitled "A Word of Exhortation to Young Friends."

In it he looked at his usual run of pressing concerns, including the evils of usury and the worship of money. Other issues hadn't been expounded on as vigorously before: he saw missionary travel now as being overdone and brings the scene alive by picturing itinerant ministers "sitting in idleness in rich Friends' rocking chairs, cracking jokes, telling anecdotes, back-biting brethren and sisters, or musing and nursing fanatical melancholy." What frames his many animadversions, though, is his belief that young Quakers of the day could, and needed to, go beyond the fractured conditions bequeathed them by the Separation. "Think then, seriously, of the importance of saving the Society," he urged his young audience. He might have been thinking of how he slowly made sense of life after the loss of his parents fully sunk in.

Hicks's feeling for young people extended beyond thoughts of the Society's future and his own youth. He was very involved in the lives of his and Sarah's five children and then their grandchildren. Their first grandchild was their daughter Susan's Phebe Ann. She arrived in 1833, when Edward was fifty-three, and became thereafter almost the center of his affections. His one portrait (other than his copy of a published

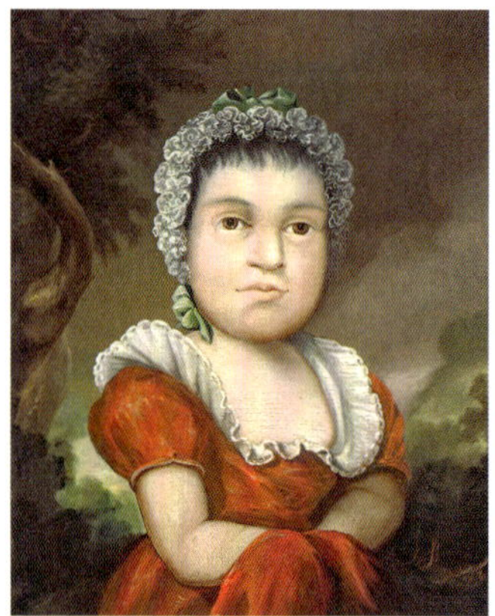

Attributed to Edward Hicks, *Portrait of a Child*, c. 1840, 17 3/8 × 14 1/2 in. (44.2 × 36.8 cm).

image of Andrew Jackson) happens to be of a child: a robust, very round-cheeked girl of about eight years old. Because there is no other painting like this by Hicks and little hard documentation linking the picture to him, the attribution is fragile, but the National Gallery, its owner, believes the painting is by Hicks, and the sitter's feisty spirit certainly recalls Edward.

For someone so concerned with childhood and youth, the verses in Isaiah surely had a special resonance. Human and animal youngsters play a much bigger role in the prophesy than one might expect. In verse 6, which introduces the subject, we are given, in addition to the "little child," a lamb, a kid, a calf, and a fatling (a young cow), and a "young lion." In the next verse, Isaiah notes that the bear and the cow are accompanied by their "young ones," and the prophet completes his scene with the child who plays near the "hole of the asp" and the child who puts "his hand on the cockatrice's den."

Before he was done with the Kingdoms, Hicks would bring all these humans and animals into his pictures plus others, young and mature, that Isaiah didn't mention. The leopard will appear occasionally with a mate, and sometimes we find a female lion attending her cubs. Some of the later Kingdoms, where we might see lambs feeding at their mother's breasts, are practically nurseries. I noted earlier that the fourth and final human figure in the series is Hebe, the Greek goddess of youth. And a young creature might be cause for confusion: it is the young lion mentioned by Isaiah. The animal Hicks repeatedly shows us, however, is light brown in color with black stripes and is occasionally (and mistakenly) referred to, because of his appearance, as a tiglon, a hybrid created by a male tiger mating with a female lion. (Many a viewer probably has wondered how a small, and always powerfully planted, tiger came on board.)

The child was Hicks's main character in his early Kingdoms. Keeping the animals relatively unchanged, he experimented with the child's sexuality and outfit, eventually turning the boy into a girl. He transformed the weaned child from a boy into a girl, too, illustrating his belief, delivered in a sermon, that there are "no sexes in souls" (and reminding us that

Krazy Kat's sexuality is also changeable). Because so many of Hicks's pictures aren't dated, it is hard to be completely sure of how he progressed, but, generalizing from the placement of the paintings in the catalogue of Miller and Mather, it appears that making the child a prepossessing and sartorially fit boy of the 1820s came early. Maybe it was scrapped because it flirted with the irreligious. In a number of other examples—in which Hicks seems to be regressing—the child is a sexually indeterminate tyke. In other works, the child, a little startlingly, is a maiden—with budding cleavage!—wearing diaphanous white, the better to see her chubby legs. She is a small classical goddess, or hostess, with her pet lion.

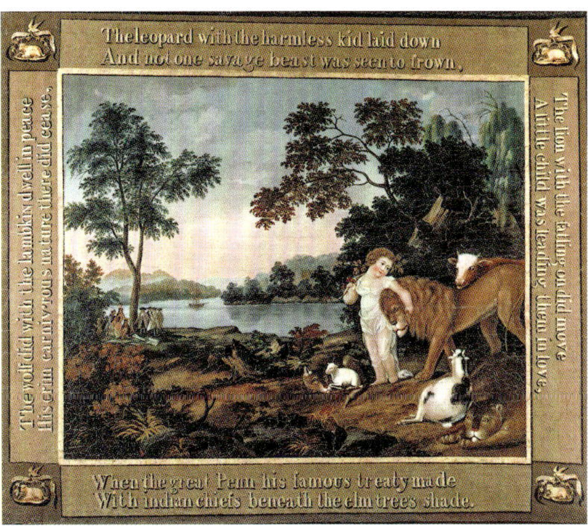

Edward Hicks, *Peaceable Kingdom*, 1826, 32 1/8 × 38 1/8 in. (81.6 × 96.84 cm).

• • •

BUT THEN, in the late 1820s and early 1830s, Hicks began making profound changes in his idea of the Kingdom—changes mirroring perhaps the unsettling Quaker terrain. The formal Separation in the Society between the factions, in 1827, brought for both sides a period of bitterness, with disownments and people leaving one meeting for another on their own accord. Then in 1830 Elias Hicks died, at eighty-two. Edward seems to have felt partially responsible for the schism, and guilty over it, and he had to have keenly experienced the loss of his renowned kinsman and friend, who was also perhaps his chief intellectual colleague. At the forefront of ministers who were appalled by the fundamentalism spreading in the Society, and forceful preachers who were much given to traveling, Elias and Edward were, respectively, the Lenin and Trotsky of the movement to keep Orthodox coarsenings at bay.

In an effort to understand why Edward continued to make *Peaceable Kingdoms* for so long, David Tatham put forth the idea that the answer had a good deal to do with Elias. In what turned out to be his final letter, in 1830, he concerned himself for the first time with the verses in Isaiah 11. This letter of Elias's, as the last word of the foremost American Friend of his day, went on to be featured in a number of Quaker publications over time; and because of it Tatham says, no doubt rightly, that the owners of *Peaceable Kingdoms* in the 1830s and 1840s would have seen a connection between the pictures and the late minister. Edward, with Elias's letter in mind, would have been given a meaningful prod to continue painting Kingdoms and a more avid audience for them.

Tatham, who in no way sought to diminish Edward's endeavor—the opposite is the case—even wondered whether it was Elias who gave Edward the idea of painting Isaiah's verses in the first place. No document has been found that can answer this or an alternate speculation—that it was Edward, who had been making paintings of the prophesy for some ten years before Elias wrote that letter, who made the older Quaker finally refer to it. Might not Elias have been indirectly saluting his cousin and intellectual comrade?

Surely Elias's importance to the Society, and the jeopardized state of Quakerdom, provided the reasons at this time for a change in the background scene of the Kingdoms. Penn and his treaty were replaced with row upon row of Quakers in suits and hats. At the apex are George Fox, Penn, and the Quaker theologian Robert Barclay. Down at the front we can find the tall Elias. Linking the group is a banner that unfurls its way through their ranks and says, "Behold I Bring You Glad Tidings of Great Joy Peace on Earth and Good Will to Men." Very tiny but quite readable, and painted in all capital letters, the banners are among the best parts of the vignette. They are like necklaces of words.

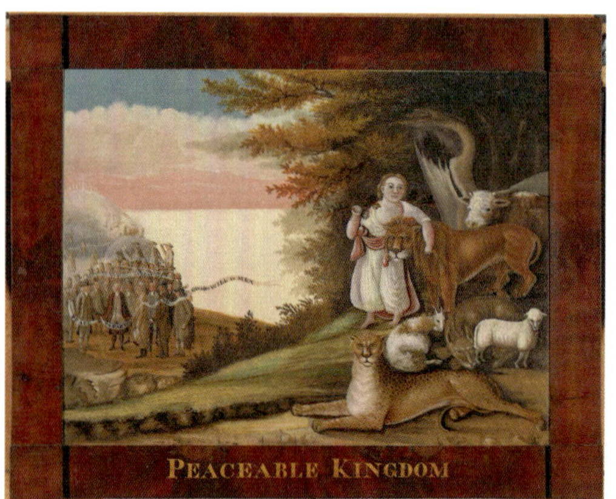

Edward Hicks, *Peaceable Kingdom*, c. 1829–30, 17 ½ × 23 ½ in. (44.5 × 59.7 cm).

The Kingdoms of these years can be remarkable, though also awkward and strange. They show Hicks breaking apart the little Richard

Westall illustration, where the carnivores are practically sedated, and making the story his own. We watch him testing options. The paintings are all considerably smaller than the border Kingdoms, possibly because he was unsure of himself. He stripped back his elaborate frames to ones with relatively simple dark brown, maple veneer, on which he added only the words "Peaceable Kingdom" (or, the uncertain speller at work, "Peacable Kingdom").

No other Kingdoms look so much like folk art. It is there principally in the child, now a girl and a rather big, immensely pantalooned, figure, who in nearly every case has the flattened, unanchored form of a folk-art creation. In the particular way that she turns her head to the side as she looks out at us, she recalls sitters in primitive portraits of the colonial era. Some of these Kingdoms also have hot pink skies—a candied and invigorating touch that would have been unimaginable in the border Kingdoms but that would not have been foreign to a primitive painter.

Was Hicks consciously taking on the manner of a naive painter? It has been suggested that at times he did so as a kind of protective covering. The argument runs that if he handled forms awkwardly he would look more like an artisan-hobbyist and less like a fine artist—and so presumably ease his conscience and limit exposing himself to censure by the greater Quaker community. Probing the issue, David Tatham shrewdly suggested about the painter's work that what "at first seems to be innocence or naivete in Hicks's style might better be seen as a willful avoidance of the appearance of sophistication."

• • •

It is undebatable that he painted in different ways. There are Kingdoms that are later in date where the leopard or wolf are so naturalistic, or so much like the work of a mainstream artist, that the effect is unnerving. On the rare times when Hicks painted horses, in late pictures of farms and of Noah's Ark, he isn't exactly naturalistic but his horses, presented in a prancing position and seemingly aware of their great size and sleek beauty, seem to come out of another, and less appealing, world of form. And when Hicks copied Sully's picture of Washington at the Delaware, he could do it in a rough-edged or folk-art-like, and quite lovely, manner (when the pictures were to be set outdoors and seen from a distance as bridge markers), or he could paint in a more conventional manner when he was making presentation pieces. And by conventional, I mean when he was copying Sully as well as he could. The results are impersonal pictures.

My sense of the changes in the Kingdoms over the years is that Hicks certainly did not switch styles at will. It is hard to imagine, given his religious and ethical ideals, that this kind of calculation—or manipulation of his audience—would have been emotionally possible for him. Likelier is that, as he became more at home with the Kingdom theme, and found that it kept calling out to him, he came to feel that a less ornate (or cosmopolitan or Neoclassical) approach was truer to the kind of quietist Quaker life he espoused. And as he continued with the theme over the years, it also makes sense that, as a highly skilled craftsman-painter, working often from illustrations in black and white of work by professional artists, he would, intentionally or not, mimic aspects of the more sophisticated styles he encountered. What dictated his continuous changes was some combination of, firstly, his evolving feelings about his congregation of characters and, secondly, the pointers on style and form that he got as he came across this or that illustration. He seems to have been in a state of experimentation all the time.

But there remains the question of why Hicks returned again and again to his Kingdom theme. Certainly, the connection with Elias and his last letter helped. The paintings themselves, however, strongly suggest that Edward kept being spurred because he realized that the pictures could be primarily about the animals, and it turned out that there were few limits to the ways he could think about—or, as it were, inhabit—them. In the roughly first decade that he made his Kingdoms, he did everything he could with his leading character, the child. He repeatedly changed the child's clothes and demeanor. He made him a her, then he made her as large as possible—and at this point he must have seen what we see: that the child was, for the moment, something of a dead end. Hicks couldn't make a breathing character out of the part.

But the animals could speak to him. And this alteration in his thinking surely stemmed from an imaginative rapport with the creatures—not from the needs of his religion. The passage in Isaiah says that a "little child shall lead them," but the words don't indicate that the child has any more significance than the beasts. It was Richard Westall, in his print, who made the child the central figure, and Hicks, in effect, outgrew Westall.

Hicks gave one account of the meaning of the animals that we see in his Kingdoms—that is to say the wild animals, those that had the most meaning for him. It came in a sermon he delivered at Goose Creek, Virginia, in February 1837. It was the year that, in August, Emerson would deliver at Harvard his "The American Scholar." That same year he was also writing a new lecture series, and in one lecture on what Robert D. Richardson, Jr., calls "intellectual integrity," Emerson could almost be drawing a conclusion about the two kinds of creatures in Hicks's pictures—a conclusion that Hicks does not spell out but that can be felt when we read his sermon or look at his Kingdoms. It is in this lecture that we hear, as Richardson puts it, "Is not our interest in genius an interest in what is wild and not tame, Emerson asks, and is not our interest in the wild an interest in what is real?"

By the time he talked at Goose Creek, Hicks had been making Kingdoms for some years where the lion, the ox, the leopard, and the other creatures had become full-bodied, distinctive presences and the child had been relegated to being little more than a sprite, usually off in a corner. The sermon, in other words, put in place conclusions about the animals that Hicks had already come to as a painter. But then the sermon isn't about the paintings. They go unmentioned, which is what we would expect from this often indirect creator. Yet we learn how the beasts had grown in Hicks's mind and why he could keep revisiting them.

Jumbled, jam-packed, and providing at times an invaluable look into Hicks's thinking, the huge Goose Creek discourse, which is longer in its present, printed form than what was delivered, reads as a warmup for the memoirs Hicks would write a number of years later. It covers, as he says, a "wide field of instruction," including his feeling for Saints Paul, Matthew, and Peter, his veneration of the early Christians, the evil of usury, and the faults he can't help noticing among Friends. The most vivid parts, though, present a kind of key to the Kingdoms. Right at the beginning Hicks refers to Isaiah's prophesy of an accord between the "wicked," flesh-eating animals and the "innocent" ones. Wanting to talk as well about the "animal body of man," he refers to the age-old notion that there are four basic human temperaments—the melancholic and the sanguine, the phlegmatic and the choleric—and that in each person one trait predominates.

Hicks's ultimate point is to wed each of Isaiah's four carnivorous beasts to one of the temperaments. He writes how when Adam was tempted in the Garden of Eden and disobeyed God, man lost his purity and his seamless unity with his maker and became calculating and self-protective. He became prey to his lower, animal nature. The word "animal" may be what prompted Hicks to bring together the Old Testament prophesy, with its four animal representatives of cruelty and selfishness, and the idea of the four temperaments, which presents a guide to man as an animal of sorts—a purely corporeal, material, unspiritual being.

In medieval physiology the temperaments are based on the predominance in the body of one humor, or fluid. Hicks, however, used as a guide what he called "the four principal elements—Earth, Air, Water, and Fire." We may think of the sanguine person, for example, as having, by definition, "blood as the predominating bodily humor" and being bloodthirsty but also confident and sturdy, and ruddy in complexion. Hicks, though, sees the sanguine person in relation to air.

Yet even though he substitutes elements for humors—and even as his linking of Isaiah's animals and the four temperaments can feel forced or arbitrary—Hicks's descriptions are such that we can see and accept his analogies. It seems suitable when he matches the person who is primarily sanguine with the leopard. An emblem of a phlegmatic person could well be the lumbering bear, and it makes sense that the choleric temperament is epitomized by the lion.

• • •

THE HICKS WHO is equally a social critic, psychologist, and observer is in his element in the passages on the wolf, representative of the melancholic temperament. With his "skulking solitary habits," the wolf, we read, "generally retires in the daytime to the inmost recesses of the swamp, or the gloomiest glens of the forest, only coming forth to prowl and devour innocent and helpless animals under cover of the darkness of night." The wolf has a "gloomy, hidden, reserved disposition"—and here Hicks leaps to the thought that this reserved disposition of wolves "enables them to keep their sorrows to themselves." That is the root of the dilemma, and the source of the strength, of the melancholic: the refusal to be, or the inability to be, forthcoming about one's sorrows.

The surprising endpoint of this subtle portrait is that Hicks sees people with "this complexion being naturally disposed to be religious." Melancholics make up the preponderance of religious people (or, as he tells it, certainly of Quakers). Equally self-protective and duplicitous, melancholics hide their fullest feelings. With their "steady, solid deportment, and very serious, solemn countenances," they "pass, as religious men and women, for more than they are worth." They carry "their religion in their faces." They are the people who reliably fill and run the temple and the church, the meeting and the mosque. They get, Hicks's words imply, no true religious ecstasy from their attendance yet they can't help but attend.

Hicks draws us in deeply with his portrayal of the melancholic temperament. It shows him at his nuanced best (and along the way he refreshes the proverbial expression a wolf in sheep's clothing), because he is far from merely condemning. He puts his finger on the terrible mixture of hypocrisy, helplessness, sense of responsibility, and inner emptiness that constitutes for him this kind of "unregenerate" person. It is the temperament that, as he sees it, produces the most suicides. Judas, he writes, was a melancholic, and so was the apostle John.

When Hicks made his first *Peaceable Kingdom* it is not likely that he had in mind the analogies between the four carnivores and the four temperaments that, many years later, he would delineate at Goose Creek. Yet perhaps he already had a sense of the wolf's character. Ostensibly, the wolf in the Cleveland picture (who bears no resemblance to the wolf in the Westall source) is a convivial creature. Openmouthed and showing his tongue, he could pass for a panting, friendly big dog. But

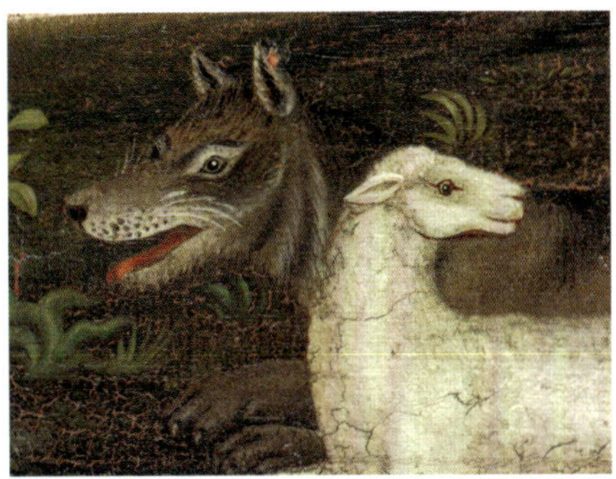

Edward Hicks, *Peaceable Kingdom*, c. 1816–18, 18 3/4 × 23 1/2 in. (47.6 × 59.7 cm), detail.

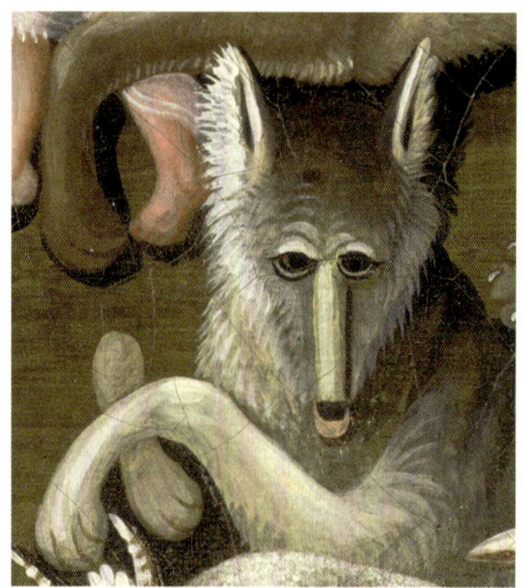

Edward Hicks, *Peaceable Kingdom*, 1832–34, 17 1/4 × 23 1/4 in. (43.8 × 59.1 cm), detail.

what is this wolf looking at? Remarkably, we cannot say. The creature could as well be masked, which might be another way of saying that melancholic—or wolfish, hypocritical—people carry "their religion in their faces." They transform their faces into masks.

As Hicks continued to paint his Kingdoms, he developed this sense of the wolf as a creature who is in hiding even as he comes before us. In classic, mature examples of the *Peaceable Kingdom*, the wolf might appear in the lower part of the orchestra, as it were, close to the picture's edge, or higher up in the stands. Wherever he is he is the least prominent of the carnivores. He generally lies on the ground, pulled up into himself. His long, bony forelegs, in an inspired touch, are drawn to his chest and slightly crossed, as if to say, daintily—a model parishioner—"Please, don't bother about me." His face is long and narrow, and his eye sockets are either darkened (as twentieth-century painters such as E. L. Kirchner, Henri Matisse, and Pablo Picasso would do it at times), or his eyes appear crossed. Occasionally we discern little, goggle eyes.

Next to the lion and the leopard, who, in their strength and beauty, invite us to join them in spirit, the wolf is resolutely unavailable. Yet for formal reasons alone he is a crucial element in the Kingdoms. His stiff and angular bodily presence, his distinctively patterned gray, white, and black colors, and the defensive gesture he makes before his chest, add notes that otherwise would be missed. In his recessive, awkward, and unhappy way he is as necessary to the Kingdoms as melancholics apparently are needed for religious organizations to function.

• • •

THE LEOPARD WAS certainly more significant to Hicks. In his earliest Kingdom, the leopard is the only animal to look at us directly, and when, some years later, as Hicks began to make the Kingdom idea more fully his own, he returned to his initial idea about the scene. In these works of the late 1820s and early 1830s, however, the leopard isn't doing anything other than glowering, or merely staring, at us, and it might be thought that Hicks didn't know what to do with the animal. But the painter possibly had a sense already that the leopard represented (among other things) some combination of mental vacancy and emotional ungroundedness.

In the sermon he gave at Goose Creek, Hicks saw the leopard as the "most subtle, cruel, restless creature, and at the same time the most beautiful of all the carnivorous animals of the cat kind." With their beauty, they all find their way to, as he put it in a wonderful phrase, "that terrible career in vanity." Hicks's leopard, the epitome of the sanguine temperament, is a kind of weathervane, sent in every direction by the air that ruled his spirit but a believer in none of them and therefore a figure of unreliability and uncenteredness.

This stunning and mercurial being is the spotted creature we find in the paintings. In the many Kingdoms done over the years, we are never sure what is going on in the leopard's head, which is quite different from the lion, whose face almost always contains a thought. Yet no creature gave Hicks so many opportunities for exquisite brushwork and color; and forever changeable and "chaffy" as Hicks calls him—the lovely, obsolete chaffy means relatively worthless—no animal is as varied a performer.

The leopard provides a welcome note of elusiveness and ungraspability to the Kingdoms. When, in the next general phase of these paintings, from about the middle 1830s, the lion moves on from being a pet of the child's and becomes—in some of Hicks's best-known pictures—a seated, practically enthroned, figure of consternation and mightiness, the leopard keeps pace with him. The leopard loses the pinched, juvenile-delinquent look he has in earlier Kingdoms, where he is eyeing us. His face fills out with a white muzzle and perfect bristling whiskers. Yet, perhaps because we know that in Kingdoms to come he will appear in other guises—and can be old in one picture and then younger in a subsequent one (unlike the lion, who gets progressively older)—the leopard doesn't seem, despite his new august bearing, to be a true figure of authority, like the lion. Essentially an actor, the leopard here is more like a retired British colonel at an officer's club, fuming over the non-delivery of his gin and tonic.

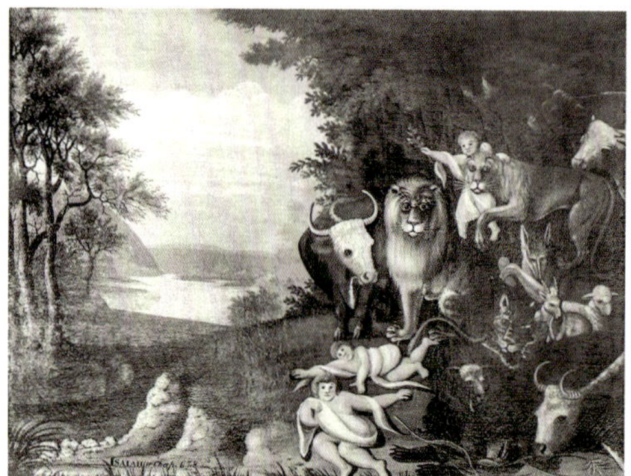

Edward Hicks, *Peaceable Kingdom*, 1829–32, 17 1/4 × 23 1/2 in. (43.8 × 59.7 cm).

The leopard inspired some of Hicks's more audacious, and comic, touches. In an amazing Kingdom that was owned by Scripps College in Claremont, California, and got lost being sent back from an exhibition in Arizona, we discover the leopard as no more than his head and a crooked paw, wedged on an angle into a space formed by the legs and rears of other animals. We can hardly believe that Hicks has taken the liberty to show the creature in so dreamlike and truncated a way (or made, in the same picture, the weaned and suckling children into large, sprawling figures enveloped in fat and rubbery swaddling clothes). In other Kingdoms, the leopard, our performer, can be seen in profile, smiling, being touched by the suckling child, or, in a marvelously silly moment, seemingly stuck up in a tree, with only his head and flopped paws visible.

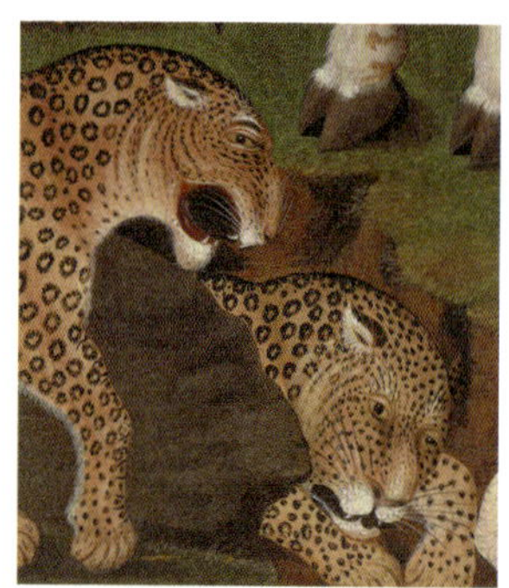

Edward Hicks, *Peaceable Kingdom*, c. 1846, 25 × 28 1/2 in. (63.5 × 72.4 cm), detail.

The goofiest of the beasts, the leopard is also the most frightening. In a remarkable small group of Kingdoms from the middle 1840s, Hicks has the leopard on his feet, with his back arched and his huge mouth wide open. He is screaming—Hicks notes that the lion roars, the wolf howls, the bear growls, and the leopard screams—and, in an unexpected change, his body can sometimes be flat up against the picture plane. At times this scary and virile cat has a mate who, though sunk in a trench, looks up with a subtle smile on her face. Then in some of the last Kingdoms the leopard is suddenly sweeter in demeanor than he has ever been and also more youthful, and his body is stretched out to preposterous lengths.

Hicks the painter obviously loved and had a lot of fun with this creature. Hicks the minister, however, needed to chastise the sanguine: as "easy prey" to drink and sensuality, they don't provide for their families and are untrustworthy, and they are likely bankrupts. But even as he moralizes Hicks draws us to these airheads, who have "more imagination than mind" and specialize in telling us what they are going to do (rather than doing anything).

As with his descriptions of the melancholic, long-faced wolf, the most engaging part of Hicks's words on the sanguine leopard come when he shows such a temperament in a religious setting. Provided they can be involved in it on their own festive terms, he says, sanguine folk are rather drawn to religion. They enjoy a good "popular mania" and brighten at the thought of "religious revivals and moral reforms." Sounding like an early incarnation of Mark Twain or Preston Sturges, he notes that the sanguine find that every "kind of business must give way to religious meetings, night meetings, camp meetings, class meetings, prayer meetings, singing meetings, temperance lectures, abolition and colonization lectures . . . where they are the most active and the most happy creatures."

In spelling out the different temperaments, with their beast avatars, Hicks, it is generally thought, had the Orthodox, whom Elias Hicks, in a letter to Edward, had loosely referred to as "beasts," in mind. But a reader of the Goose Creek sermon feels this only slightly. Whether his subject is the melancholic, professionally pious wolf or the sanguine, sensationalistic leopard, Hicks, one senses, is writing about Quakers in general—people in general, really. (For the record, Eleanore Price Mather noted that "though Quakerism has many wolves, it has few leopards.")

Hicks the preacher is less involving on the bear, perhaps because when he considered the phlegmatic temperament his subject wasn't religious life. Taking off from our sense of this creature as an assiduous gatherer of foods for winter's hibernation, he saw the bear—"cold and unfeeling . . . dull and inert"—as a representative of people who believe chiefly in the slow, steady accumulation of money. They are, it follows, the money lenders, or usurers, the group guaranteed to send Hicks into a tizzy. Not hypocrites, though, like the calculatingly solemn wolves, or vain like the chaffy leopards, the plodding, impersonal bears don't excite the Hicks who was a sharp-eyed social critic. They chiefly prod Hicks the tiresome ranter.

Yet the bear is a quietly necessary presence in the paintings. One invariably wants to seek out both his malleable, big, black shape, which Hicks got from printed sources and then periodically altered, and the creature's stylized face, whose color and pattern Hicks invented. The bear's face is a matter of his black head coming to a point with an orange-tan muzzle, with the same color used for markers over his eyes and the inside of his little rounded ears. His mouth is open, showing a red tongue and tiny white teeth. Often we see him about to chew an ear of corn. These few strong colors and how they are placed together form an almost abstract zone that is a pleasure to see in itself.

• • •

IN HIS SERMON, Hicks spent even less time on the choleric temperament. Although some commentators believe that he identified with the leopard, he says that he saw himself, and was "ashamed almost to think of" himself, in the fiery lion, a proud, power-hungry creature, prone to anger and "impatient of contradiction." Perhaps because of this, Hicks doesn't, at least in his sermon, get under the skin of the lion, as he does the wolf and the leopard. He doesn't make the lion a character. His effort goes rather to showing how anger is not in itself sinful but can be a form of grace in advance. It can lead to our asking for forgiveness for our intemperateness. Saint Paul, he feels, was inherently of a fiery, choleric nature.

In his paintings, however, Hicks rarely fails to make the lion a character. From the earliest Kingdom, the lion's spirit and expression were more graspable, and human, than those of any other figure, including the child's. In the Kingdoms of the early 1830s the animal comes even more fully into his own, and the paintings become the works we generally recognize as *Peaceable Kingdom*s.

The most dramatic change is that the lion is now seated and turns his head left, to look at us. The pose, we read, goes back to late medieval times and is chivalric in origin. A seated lion, turned to look in our or some other direction, is, to take a well-known example, one of the companions of the aristocratic young woman in the fifteenth-century tapestry cycle *The Lady and the Unicorn*. Hicks, it is thought, came upon the seated lion by being familiar with local tavern and inn signs, which themselves kept alive types of representations going back centuries. However he developed the pose, this new lion, independent of the child, was probably crucial to his attaining in his pictures an emotionality and a feeling for form and composition that he had not achieved before.

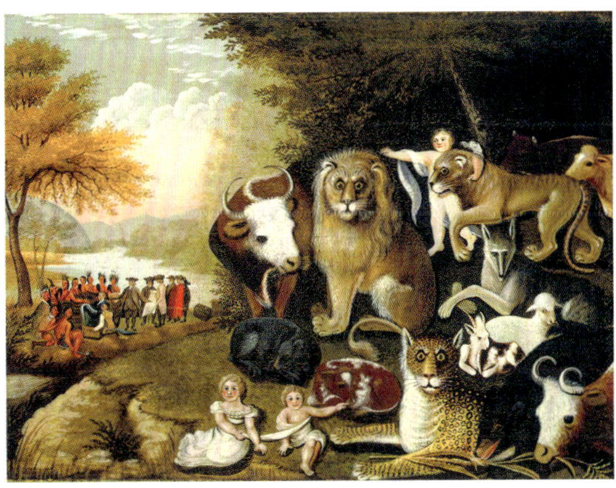

Edward Hicks, *Peaceable Kingdom*, c. 1833–34, 17 7⁄16 × 23 9⁄16 in. (44.3 × 59.8 cm).

In the paintings that were undoubtedly done first and are the more remarkable ones, the lion is tense, demonic, and frightening. When one thinks of Hicks as a painter of animals whose stares can practically bore holes in us, these are the pictures in which he does it. The large pupils are in the center of large, round irises firmly encircled by black, creating figures—the leopards have similar eyes—that hover between a play-acting scariness and the genuinely disturbing. The reason for the alarmed state, we read, was the recent upheaval in the Society of Friends, when the Orthodox removed themselves to create their own meetings. Describing the lion in the Brooklyn Museum's superlative example of these pictures, Mather succinctly noted that he is "riven by the guilt and fear that came in the wake of the Separation."

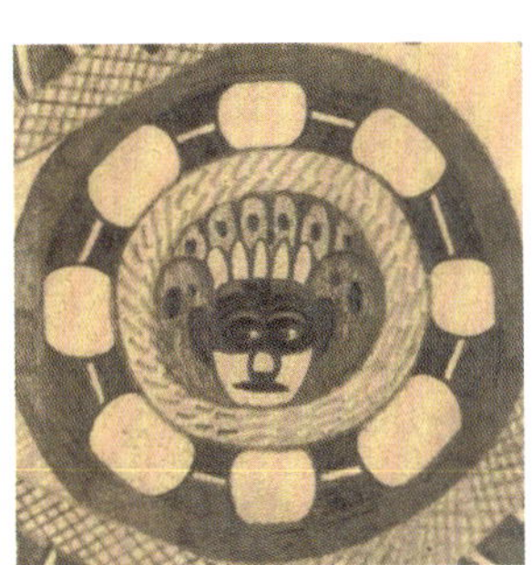

Adolf Wölfli, *St. Adolf – Ring of Oberburg*, 1918, 19 1⁄2 × 27 in. (49.5 × 68.6 cm), detail.

Carolyn Weekley caught the full flavor of the situation when, referring to the lion and the leopard, she added that, "Neither at peace nor angry, they exude energy and appear ill at ease and somewhat startled. Their poses suggest a tenuous peace, a delicate balance of difficult and unresolved issues." With their outlandishly bristling demeanors, Hicks's lions have an antic power that makes them, I believe, more alive to us than all the handsome, wounded, or lordly stallions, tigers, and lions seen in the roughly contemporaneous pictures of Géricault and Eugène Delacroix.

Hicks's hypnotic animals can even seem funny. A viewer acquainted with the work of Adolf Wölfli might be reminded, looking at these lions, of the Swiss artist's alter ego: a little face in a black burglar's mask whose big eyes dart about through the openings and who is as charming as he is creepy. Mather caught something of this underlying zaniness when she called the Brooklyn lion a "clown among lions, aghast at himself yet, withal, amused."

After making a few of these amazing pictures, where the lion could be a criminal—or merely overly frazzled—Hicks must have realized he had to move on. Keeping the lion seated but softening his eyes and his electrified manner, Hicks created a new character: the lion as presiding authority, the group's slightly wary CEO. Even after he is no longer seated, this is the role, with many variations, and with a few important exceptions, that the lion would play from here on in.

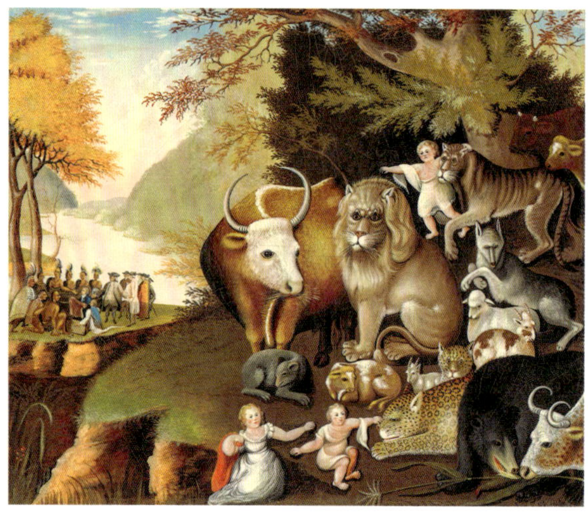

Edward Hicks, *Peaceable Kingdom*, c. 1834, 29 5⁄16 × 35 1⁄2 in. (74.5 × 90.1 cm).

If the seated-lion pictures have been especially admired—Weekley believes that some of them were the "most sophisticated" Kingdoms Hicks did—it may have to do with the form of the lion. Seated, he feels enthroned, which befits a "kingdom." Seated, he is seen with only his left front and left back legs visible, which is almost as important as his kingship. His position emphasizes his flatness as a form and his compact, triangular shape.

On his haunches, the lion is a particularly folk-art-like figure, and the pictures have a folk-art flatness in their entirety. Perhaps because he was working in this spirit, Hicks arranged his many characters with a seeming ease, and his arrangements accordingly have a quickly perceived clarity and sense of balance. All the participants seem to be set out in their most readable positions. The spatial lucidity must be what Weekley meant by the sophistication of these pictures.

When Hicks in subsequent Kingdoms put the lion on his feet again, it was as if he had passed beyond the folk-art phase of his self-education. He never went back to the seated lion, and he rarely again conveyed the sense of animals neatly stacked in place. This is not to say that he no longer made forms or treated space in ways that bespeak folk art. In Kingdoms from around 1836 and 1837, in which we see the lion now on all fours, Hicks can make the creature's head and body preternaturally massive. Yet showing the lion on all fours meant that there was space—air—under him. With this the paintings almost automatically became somewhat naturalistic, and Hicks in a sense no longer had a folk-art flatness as a guide. He was, as an artist skilled in the handling of paint, but not in naturalistic drawing, in virgin terrain.

In the later Kingdoms we watch him playing with how realistic he wants details to be. Sometimes he paints the children or the kid in such assuredly offhanded and abbreviated ways that his brushwork recalls the sketch style of European master painters. For a string of works he shows all the children as bald, dressed up, tiny adults. Alighting weightlessly here and there among the animals, they are like so many exotic toys belonging to these creatures. They might be versions of the dwarfs that in earlier times were kept at European courts.

• • •

THE LION OF the later Kingdoms is generally seen in profile, looking left. He is the anchor of nearly every picture, but sometimes he is not fully there mentally. He can seem preoccupied. The most absorbing of the later lions are those where his position has changed entirely, and he is coming directly out at us. Hicks, it is thought, derived aspects of this lion from an illustration in a contemporary Bible, itself possibly based on Flemish sources indebted to Rubens, for the story of Daniel in the Lion's Den. Hicks seems to have been most drawn to the way the lion's body is elongated and his head is lower to the ground than the rest of him. He used this taut bodily position to create a stooped, lurching, and haggard being.

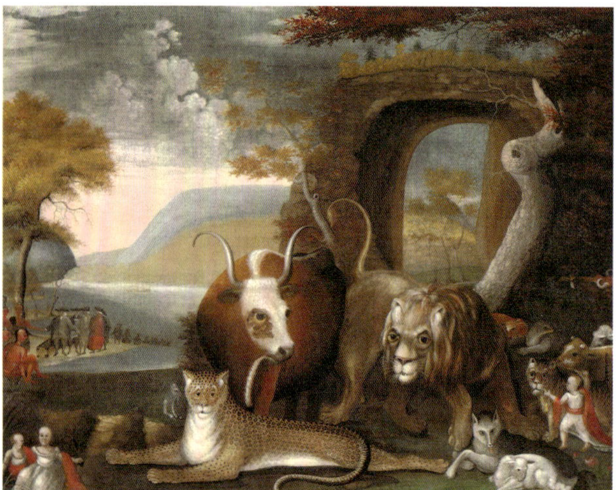

Edward Hicks, *The Peaceable Kingdom and Penn's Treaty*, 1845, 24 1/4 × 31 in. (61.6 × 78.7 cm).

The elongated lion is the central player in what appear in reproduction to be a number of affecting and dynamic Kingdoms. One of the few such works that the public can see belongs to the Yale University Art Gallery—it was a gift of the great-grandson of the artist—and it is certainly a masterpiece. One looks at a picture pervaded by dark blue, punctuated by passages of vibrant white which, on the ox's head and the ridge on his chest and back, on the leopard's chest and belly, and on the lion's knowing, old-person's face, jump out at the viewer.

It could be nighttime—a night full of flying clouds—although one feels this more in front of the picture than when seeing it reproduced. Instead of his usual forest background, Hicks has inserted Virginia's Natural Bridge, which he initially took from Henry Tanner's map and used in a number of early paintings. The bridge's archlike opening to more sky suggests that the scene is taking place in a ruin, and the setting helps make the animals and the vaguely extraterrestrial, yet appealing children seem as if they could be a homeless crowd gathering on a windy night in a safe, overlooked corner. The old, dead tree, which leans back, is the perfect wrecked guardian for what could be an assembly of outcasts.

The centerpiece of this powerful work is the lion. He is a figure of grandeur and decrepitude. His body seems close to collapse. His springs are shot. Bringing the lion to the ground wasn't, however, only about noting the animal's aged presence. Hicks in his later pictures was increasingly concerned with separating the lower and upper parts of his scenes. He was changing the structure, and the nature of the drama, of his Kingdoms, and he was at the same time beginning to evolve new subjects. It was a good if challenging place for a man in his mid-sixties to be.

An Open Door

Life changed for Hicks in the 1840s. Always plagued by colds and coughing—he believed he had pulmonary consumption—he was now becoming deaf and feeling himself an old man. He was well aware of the Biblical definition of a person's lifespan being some seventy years. He apparently expected that such would be his life's duration and, roughly, it was. The thought made him feel particularly close to his past and his posthumous existences, and, in addition, he knew that his fellow Quakers expected him, especially as a nationally known minister, to bring forth a journal account of his life. There were now pressing reasons to think about himself, an activity he guiltily knew he excelled at. After going ahead and writing (though not publishing) his memoirs at age sixty-four, he found himself ready to put the same energy into the diary that he started at sixty-six.

Death, unsurprisingly, plays a leading role in the diary (which it did not in his memoirs). Already in its second sentence he is recording the deaths of "several of my particular friends and acquaintances," and the sheer number of deaths he faced or heard about in a year, though perhaps not wildly unusual for a nineteenth-century person, would for most of us be crushing. Of course, he knew about or attended many of these passings in his capacity as a minister. He was invited to the funeral of Jacob Smith, for instance, by the man's "youngest daughter, who was quite a little girl at the death of her mother, whose funeral I attended ten or twelve years ago."

But there seems to have been a fine line between the deaths of personal friends and of Quakers he knew as a minister. The references to mortality are mesmerizingly copious. "I attended Isaac's funeral at Horseham . . . Yesterday Benjamin Swain, of Bristol, was buried . . . This day attended the funeral of Rachel Heston . . . was invited to attend the funeral of Elisha Wilkinson . . . Heard of the death of Daniel Stroud . . . I have heard of the death of one of the companions of my youth, Margaret Richardson . . . Heard of the death of Aaron Eastburn, a goodly Orthodox Friend . . . of William Brown, a poor colored young man . . . Received the affecting account of the death of Joseph Davis' wife, Ellen . . . Oh! How I felt for her dear husband and children . . . I was this day invited to the funeral of my poor neighbor Charles Buckman . . . Spoke of the funeral of another of my neighbors, John Ettinger, a young store keeper . . . I attended the funeral of Susan Cadwallader . . . Spoke of the funeral of Elizabeth Buckman, wife of Charles, that was buried last week, which appeared to bring a tendering solemnity over the meeting. In the afternoon attended the funeral of Benjamin Dyer."

The above took place over the course of some three months. It does not represent all the deaths and funerals he noted in this time. May of 1846 continued in the same vein: "Received two invitations to funerals" —that was on the 4th. The next day: "Just returned from the funeral of our dear friend Mary Knowles." Sometimes he would be asked to speak at funerals of people he didn't know. "Had an invitation to attend the funeral of a woman by the name of Carr, at Wrightstown, an entire stranger." He wondered at the "propriety of going." Was he, he thought (in a passage I admit I do not fully comprehend), merely stroking his ego in "preaching at funerals"? But he saw a reason for going: "Is there not something like an open door, when a special invitation is sent to me by a stranger?"

The death notices continued. There are too many names to give more than a sampling here; and his work as a gravedigger for his meeting meant that he was acquainted with loss even when not asked to speak. (With the view from his house of the meeting and adjacent cemetery, he would have faced the topic regularly even if he had not been a minister.) In thinking about Friends who had died, and recollecting moments as a gravedigger, he wrote with particular feeling about Hannah Parker.

He knew her from the days when she was a child and would unobtrusively attend the first Friends services held in Newtown by herself, her parents being Presbyterian. As she grew she came to dress like a Friend, and in time was accepted into membership of the meeting. Ultimately, Hannah Parker became a minister, and a forthright and admired one. More than Edward, though, she was overtaken by pulmonary consumption and "her poor body was . . . a mere shadow." Her life, he wrote, "would furnish rich materials to a ready writer, for a memorial that might be worth reading—as for me, I can only give a rough sketch."

This proximity to mortality could at times lay him low. "Nothing worth recording," he wrote at one point, "excepting my serious thoughtfulness of death and eternity, which I have reason to look for daily, if not hourly. Oh! It will be an awful thing to die." No thoughts of his own demise, however, could compare with the wound he received, strangely enough, some two weeks after beginning his diary. It was late February and very cold, with "much snow in the roads." Early March turned out to have the coldest and snowiest weather he could remember for that time of year. It was the background for the roughest news he had received, possibly ever: the illness and soon the death of "my favorite, my darling"—his thirteen-year-old grandchild, Phebe Ann Carle, who lived with her family in New York City.

"I have wept, I have prayed—what can I do more? I have never known what such sorrow was before," he wrote that early March in the aftermath of his grandchild's death. Later he said that he went through the "most intense suffering for ten days I ever experienced," and continuing references to Phebe Ann in the year's diary suggest that his grief abated only slightly.

How capable, observant, and sensitive she could be, and how her passing could make so deep a mark on Edward and the rest of her family, can be sensed in letters of hers quoted by Alice Ford—as when she wrote, at twelve, "Mrs. Stewart invited us to spend the evening with her last week to eat some of her own make of Ice Cream. There was to be no one there but us. They have the most books I ever saw in one house, and one is eight hundred years old. It is a great curiosity. It was written with a pen before the invention of printing. The ink looks as black as if it had been done a few days since. They have several from two hundred to six hundred years old, and five or six of the most beautiful drawings I ever looked upon." She went on, "Please write soon, for I do like to receive a long letter from Newtown."

A year after her death Edward needed to note the occasion in his diary. Shortly after that he gave up his daily record, possibly because his now increasingly limited energies were going into his painting. He never mentions his painting in the diary, but he regularly notes his being at work, or in his shop, or doing his "business." Whatever he was busy with, it was the cause of a "singular thing": he was supposed to go to the funeral of Elizabeth Buckman, but he was so "intent on my work" that he missed the gathering at her house. He thought he could just as well meet up with everyone at the graveyard close to his shop, so he continued working. The next time he asked his son about when the "funeral was coming, I was told that it had come and gone. I was really astonished. . . ."

• • •

CONSIDERING THE AMOUNT of painting that Hicks did in the last four or five years of his life, it is odd that he recorded only one occasion when he lost track of his ministerial duties. His dwelling on his past and opinions in his memoir and diary, and the biting, incessant presence of death in these years, together seem to have given him a new awareness. Perhaps he saw it as being, as he said of the funeral of the unknown woman in Wrightstown, "something like an open door, when a special invitation is sent." Whether or not he saw the making of easel pictures as a "special invitation," his art seems to have absorbed him in a way that it had not done so before. Although in the many previous years he generally did not sign or date his paintings, he now regularly did so. With a sense of ego that hardly seems Quakerlike, he would stencil (on the back) those done in 1847, say, as being "Painted by E. Hicks in the 68th year of his age." On the one time I was able to see the back of a later Kingdom I was struck by the care and assertiveness with which the frame's rear side had been painted a dark green, with the large lettering done in black.

He returned to Sully's image of Washington at the Delaware, making some of these late versions as big as four feet across. There were experiments—not half-hearted but, judging from reproductions, not successes, either—with entirely new images. He made forays into the

Old Testament story of David and Jonathan; a scene from *The Tempest* (whose authenticity has been questioned); and a landscape with Native Americans hunting a jaguar. Finally getting around to forebears in the realm of animal painting, he tried his hand at a number of relatively small-size canvases, indebted to prints of Dutch seventeenth-century painters, of cattle and sheep.

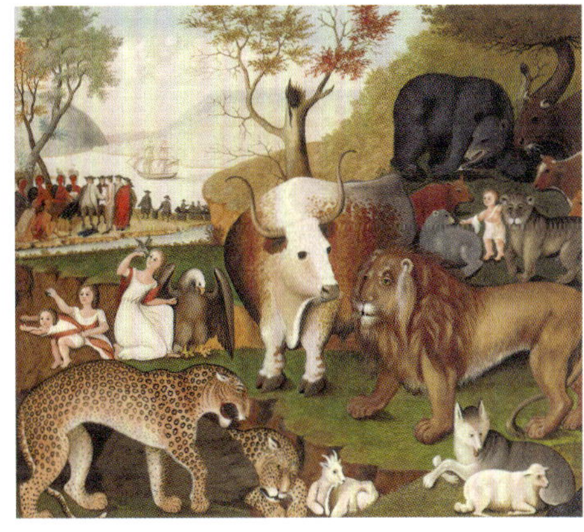

Edward Hicks, *Peaceable Kingdom*, c. 1846, 25 × 28 ½ in. (63.5 × 72.4 cm).

Far more notable was Hicks's exploration of new ways of handling his Kingdoms. With the freedom of a trained artist in his or her prime—and quite unlike a folk artist—he took almost each new version as an opportunity to come up with a different conception of his troupe of characters and of the grassy stage they assemble on. In the great Kingdom in the de Young museum, he was working, unusually, with an almost square canvas. Was that the reason behind the particular monumentality of this picture, where the lion, ox, and screaming leopard are almost equally big and each comes toward the others in the center? Or perhaps Hicks chose this nearly square canvas because he had an arrangement like this in mind beforehand.

Edward Hicks, *Peaceable Kingdom with the Leopard of Serenity*, c. 1846–48, 26 × 29 ½ in. (66 × 75 cm).

In another late Kingdom with the same nearly square format, his composition is almost entirely the opposite. The power of this picture lies in its breadth and its brilliantly coordinated multifariousness; it represents a virtuoso piece of planning and looks in reproduction far bigger than its actual dimensions of little more than two feet square.

Hicks has made almost every being in it if not the actual same size then equal in impact, from the lion down to the children.

He has turned his setting into an amphitheater. Each character has breathing room, and the forest has been cleared out entirely. The few trees that are left seem thriving and moribund at the same time, and with their twisting trunks, luxuriant foliage, and spiky dead zones, they are as much personages as any of the creatures, whose own ranks are swelling. Their number now includes a family of sheep, with a mother nursing a lamb (they exist independently of our original sheep, who nestles alongside the wolf). Yet with all this equality and influx there is little sense of clogging or stasis. What we look at is more like a game board with every piece in play. And how sweet to find the leopard's stretched-out rear leg touching the elbow of the wolf. Neither seems aware of it.

The magnificent late Kingdom in the Phillips Collection casts an entirely different spell. Here the forest is back, and we can look deep into it. Lone trees carry less weight than the foliage, especially the superlative painting of red and brown leaves that cover much of the scene and give the picture its note of a November afternoon around four, when the light starts to go down fast. This Kingdom also stands out because it is one of the first where Hicks was attempting to create a new kind of drama, one where there was less sense of rank and hierarchy among the animals and more importance given to the upper, seemingly empty reaches of the scene—to sky and light.

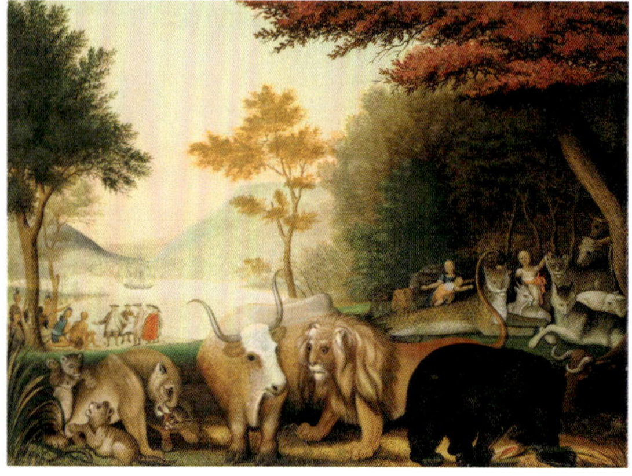

Edward Hicks, *Peaceable Kingdom*, 1845–46, 24 1/8 × 32 1/8 in. (61.3 × 81.6 cm).

In the Phillips painting, the lion, as usual, is the only creature registering some larger awareness: he is clearly uneasy, maybe even apprehensive. He carries an overcast state of feeling that one hardly sees in American art before the portraits Eakins made, beginning in the late 1880s, of Edith Mahon, Amelia C. Van Buren, and other women who face us stoically, or turn away in resignation. But the larger note of the Kingdom in Washington is of a settledness and serenity, and it comes as much from the novel way Hicks has engineered the scene as from its sorrel and burgundy tones. He has made the lion, ox, bear, and lioness with her cubs all roughly the same size, and brought them, in an overlapping row, down to the lip of the stage—where they form a kind of foundation or platform for everything else.

In his five or so last years, Hicks's art has a lot to do with horizontality in itself and with how to make the bottom of a picture its populated part. He appears to be saying in his Kingdoms that relations between his characters were of less concern to him than the need to get them moving—moving from their forest enclave out to a wider, brighter somewhere else. There were spiritual and psychological connotations to this. One believes that the corporeal world was loosening its hold on him, and that what he called, in the last words of his diary, the "Heaven of Heavens" was increasingly real. But the shift in his approach came with no signs of an overtly symbolic nature, and it clearly stimulated his artistry. He found ways to show this shift in his last Kingdoms and in subjects he had never tried before: the grave of William Penn, farms and farm life, Noah's Ark. He was going on to a new stage in his art.

• • •

NO DOUBT BECAUSE he was keeping company with death daily, Hicks was drawn, in 1847, to the subject of Penn's burial site in Jordans, England. The gentle, fine works he came up with may be a cut above the pictures of Penn's treaty with the Lenape tribe because those paintings are crowded with Hicks's standard-issue folk-art human beings while the scenes of Penn's grave have few of these dubious figures to contend with. (On the other hand, the variety of strong colors in the treaty paintings gives them a more vibrant presence on the wall.)

Hicks's inspiration for his gravesite pictures was a recent print of an eighteenth-century Dutch painting, which he never saw (and which happened all the while to be in Philadelphia). The print shows the easily overlooked grave before a house. Out beyond its walled-off ground is a leafy, hilly landscape, and toward the bottom there is a path with a cow and some sheep moseying along. This element may have been part of what caught Hicks's eye. In the half-dozen versions he made of this scene, it is the element that he kept changing. He made the animals more important and added as their leader a massive, and very horizontally shaped, bull.

The striking aspect of the gravesite pictures, though, is the house—and here it should be said that Hicks in his last five or so years was juggling a number of new issues, and for a moment I want to set aside his concern with horizontality. The first time I saw one of his pictures of Penn's grave I was irritated by the ghostly colorlessness and stage-set-like flatness of the building and its surrounding wall, certainly as compared with the rest of the scene. Yet Hicks was clearly taken by the chance of showing structures this way, and I have come to appreciate it because of how he developed it in his farm paintings, which he was also doing in his last years. There are some half dozen pictures of farms, and a crucial aspect of these scenes are the buildings, whether farmhouses, barns, or sheds, and the fences and walls.

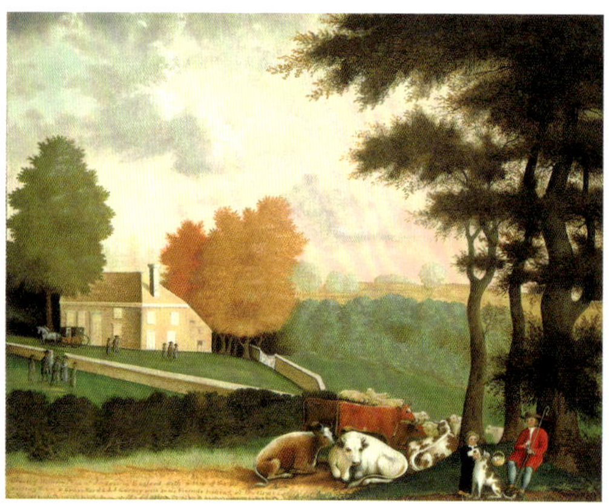

Edward Hicks, *The Grave of William Penn*, c. 1847–48, 23 3⁄4 × 29 3⁄4 in. (60.4 × 75.5 cm).

• • •

THE FARM PAINTINGS, however, claim our attention for many reasons. They are Hicks's best-known (or most reproduced) works outside of his Kingdoms—though even folk art specialists might not know that they are different from everything else he did and came as part of a late transformation of his art. His farm pictures are reproduced from time to time not only for what they say about Edward Hicks but because they seem to contain our fonder thoughts about rural life and the farmsteads of the past. Not that Hicks consciously sought to show this, but his pictures present the most resonant images we have about the era when farming life and the family farm were practically synonymous with the young

American republic—when the representative figure of the new nation was the informed, independent-minded yeoman farmer, the citizen cultivating his land to feed his wife and children.

But the pictures tell even more about the national endeavor in the antebellum era, because in his last two paintings of the subject Hicks gives us a glimpse of the speculative business that farming eventually became. In a handful of pictures, in other words, he encompassed both the appealing story of the farmer creating his own compact universe and the newer realities of agrarian life.

The paintings are all of actual Bucks County properties, named in the titles. The earliest ones were (as the titles have it) of the Hillborn and Twining residences—there are four similar versions of the latter—and present prosperous gentlemen farmers in their well-ordered domains. We see farmhouses and farmyards, barns and livestock. Mr. Hillborn, presumably, is tilling in the one painting, and Mr. Twining (the painter's adoptive father, the reader will remember) stands by his wife and looks out at his smoothly humming realm in the other work.

Although small aspects of the paintings derive from one source or another (a man getting on a horse, in the Twining scene, comes from Sully's painting of General Washington), the pictures are original Hicks compositions. This makes more notable the canny organization and fullness of these canvases (particularly of the Twining image), which adeptly bring together, with breathing room and a sense of organic rightness, details that probably could not all be in one place as we see them. There are cows, horses, and sheep with their young, and farmhands at their chores. Fences, exquisitely sited single trees, and numerous subsidiary buildings all have their place. Some folks are mounting up,

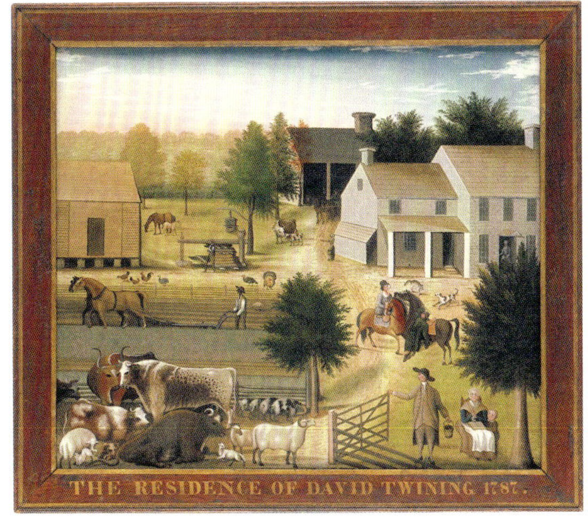

Edward Hicks, *The Twining Residence*, 1845–47, 26 1/2 × 31 9/16 in. (67.3 × 80.2 cm).

perhaps getting ready to go to town, and, although it is not evident in every reproduction, there is a lineup of pigs at a trough, their tails, as Mather put it, a "phalanx of apostrophes."

In describing the contemporaneous paintings of George Durrie, which show farmhouses and barns—and oxen carting cut wood, and sleighs arriving through the snowy roads—James Thomas Flexner used, perfectly, the word "contentment" to say what the Connecticut artist's delicately rendered pictures are about. The word would suit Hicks's earth-toned and more interestingly detailed portraits of the Hillborn and especially the Twining residences. But a grander thought than contentment is needed for Hicks's last two farm pictures. They represent another class of work.

Showing buildings, people, and animals as aspects of expansive, sky-filled landscapes, the later paintings—of the Cornell farm, from 1848, and of the Leedom farm, from the following year—are epic in concept and spirit. They aren't about the farm as an extension of one's home. They are about farming as an enterprise. At four feet or so on a side, they are physically larger than all but a handful of pictures that Hicks had done before. Their very existence, coming on top of the various paintings of Penn and Washington and Niagara—and even of the Kingdoms—attests to Hicks's

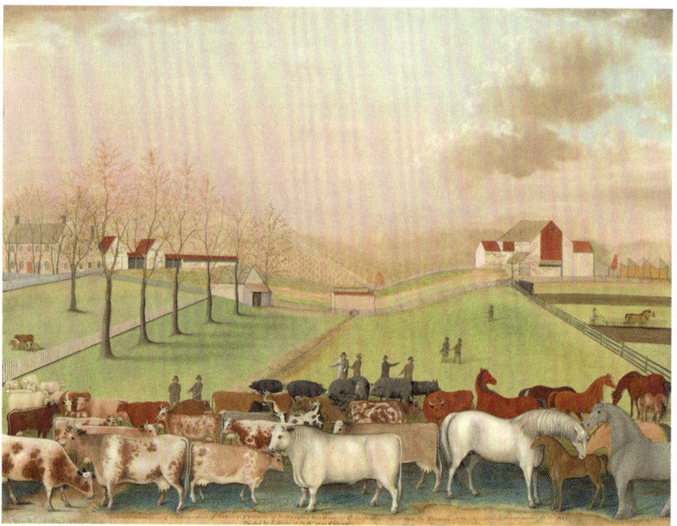

Edward Hicks, *The Cornell Farm*, 1848, 36 ¾ × 49 in. (93.3 × 124.4 cm).

extraordinary ambition as an artist. It never let up. It was growing still in 1849, which he rightly expected would be his last year. His painting of the Cornell farm is a more audacious work than his slightly earlier scenes of the Twining residence, and then in his view of the Leedom farm he possibly surpassed the Cornell painting.

The picture of James Cornell and a number of other small figures, his prize livestock, and, in the distance, his fields and houses—seen in, its inscription says, an "Indian summer view"—is the better known of the two late farm scenes. This is partly because it is in the National Gallery and so is seen by more people and reproduced more often—it forms the jacket of the Gallery's important 1992 catalogue, *American Naive Painting*—than the Leedom farm scene, which is somewhat buried in the Abby Aldrich Rockefeller Folk Art Museum in Williamsburg, Virginia. But the Cornell picture also catches our attention quickly. It is a highly singular work.

Certainly, next to most American landscapes of the era, with their Hudson River school taste for varnished surfaces, dark brown terrains, big clumps of generic trees, and technicolor skies, and even next to scrappier folk art landscapes of the moment, Hicks's picture is idiosyncratic. In memory, it is a pale green scene with red notes here and there, and its

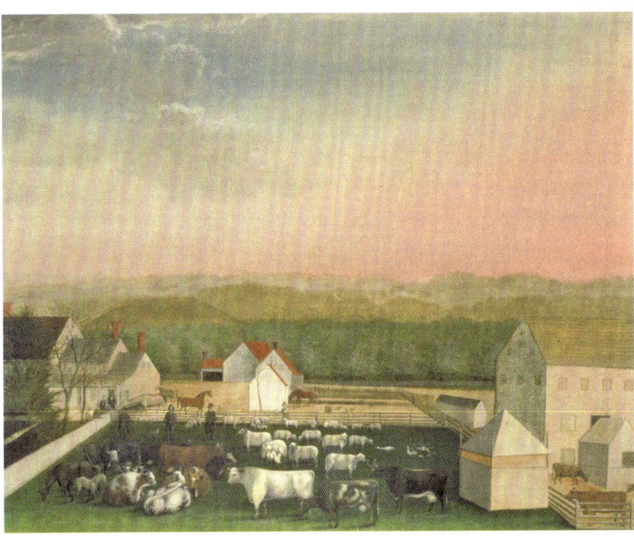

Edward Hicks, *Leedom Farm*, 1849, 40 1/8 × 49 1/16 in. (101.9 × 124.6 cm).

picture construction is at once awkward and elegant. It asks to be viewed as if it were a scroll. We automatically look first at the painting's traffic jam of cattle, horses, and big, black pigs at the lower edge of the canvas. As our eyes move up, we find small gesticulating men in the fields, a pleasingly rigid row of leafless trees, an undulating layer of delicate buildings and walls, and finally a big, pale sky.

The picture is seemingly placid and immobile, yet it makes us continually readjust to its sloping and rising terrain. But it also has the impalpability of a watercolor, and this is not the case with the painting of David Leedom's farm, which provides, in its lustrous substantiality, a richer experience. This is a view from a great distance of a precisely ordered world on, as its inscription says, a May morning. Its core is Leedom's cattle and sheep, set out one by one on an expanse of glowing green grass, which is sheltered by farm structures of every description. Beyond are softly blended trees and then misty hills and finally a vast, peachy pink sky. Perhaps because of the immensity of the space we encounter, and the eye-focusing way the mostly bone-white animals are displayed on the grass—rather like jewelry placed on a jeweler's small presentation tray—the Leedom farm painting has the quality of an enveloping vision.

The artificiality of the picture's many buildings and walls, which resemble the screens used as partitions in a Japanese interior, adds to the work's distinctiveness. The structures in all the farm paintings (and in the versions of the grave of William Penn) strike the same artificial note, and it grows on one. These drawing-like areas—they make us think of pencils and rulers—form an enlivening counterpoint to the parts of the pictures that show trees, animals, and everything else.

The buildings have little color, though the brick chimneys, and sometimes the roofs and barn sidings, are red, and the play of red, white, and tan on the roofs and walls of the buildings on the hill in the Cornell painting is a confectionary delight. It makes this part of the picture as lively as the bottom, where the many animals are. These architectural details are roughly true to rural Pennsylvania design. In *Mahantango Valley Farm,* for instance, a late nineteenth-century naive painting in the National Gallery (by an unnamed artist), one finds the same red roofs, tall narrow structures, and severely plain facades. But Hicks emphasizes the sheer paleness—sometimes the stark whiteness—of his buildings.

The intangibility that he was presenting might have a religious meaning for him. Perhaps Hicks was suggesting the immateriality of this world, as opposed to the next. Or are we, as we take in the balsa-wood weightlessness of these structures, being given a foretaste of heavenly mansions? Or was it that Hicks didn't want to be, or could not be, conventionally naturalistic about sheds, barns, or walls, and decided to stylize them—and found that as he worked in this manner it became increasingly pleasurable?

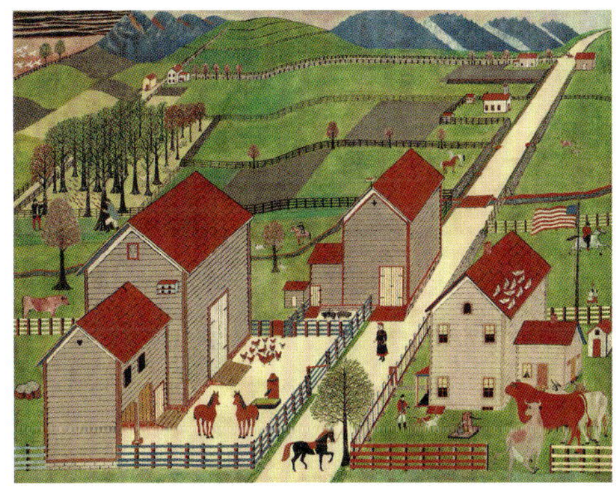

Unknown American artist, *Mahantango Valley Farm*, late nineteenth century, 28 × 36 5⁄16 in. (71.1 × 92.2 cm).

• • •

GIVEN THAT IN the first half of the nineteenth century, the country's economy was largely built on farming, the little that American painters made of it can seem odd, and it comes as a surprise that Hicks in his few images accounted for it as well as anybody. Primitive painters, who generally lived in countrysides marked primarily by farms, tended to tackle the theme more than professional painters, but no one folk artist appears to have delved into the subject—and this makes a kind of sense. The clientele for "country" portraits undoubtedly felt little need for pictures of farms for their parlors when farming scenes hit them from every side once they stepped outside the door.

For William Sidney Mount, the foremost painter of everyday moments in America in the 1830s and 1840s, the country's agrarian existence was little more than a backdrop. We see field hands taking breaks from haying, a nicely dressed yeoman with his scythe, and men chatting by a barn. The barn was Mount's favorite setting. But for him it had almost nothing to do with farming. He saw it as a theater stage. His subject was music and the dancing that went on in or just outside a barn—that and the chance a barn gave him to paint another favorite subject: wood boards. Winslow Homer was tempted by the theme of farming life probably as much as any nineteenth-century American painter, though he didn't go into it more deeply than Mount. By the time Homer showed his Civil War veteran working in a wheat field with a scythe, or painted farm hands shyly courting shy milkmaids in the 1870s, the independent, yeoman farmer already stood for an earlier, more innocent America.

It is commonly thought that the Civil War, with its military need for heavy industry, marked the end of agriculture's centrality to the US economy. But even before manufacturing began to transform the country, farming was beginning to be reorganized on business lines. As Richard Hofstadter wrote in *The Age of Reform*, the "shift from self-sufficient to commercial farming"—or the way that the farmer's concern went from no more than feeding his family to contemplating his cash crop—was "complete in Ohio by about 1830." Other states were not long in witnessing the same story.

Hicks was literally thinking of the past with his pictures of David Twining's farmstead. They are set according to their titles in 1785 and 1787, when Edward, who we see leaning against the wide lap of the seated Elizabeth Twining, who rests her Bible there, was a boy. And while his painting of the Cornell and Leedom farms are set in the present of the late 1840s, they, too, have, at least to our eyes now, a retrospective air about them. Hicks probably didn't conceive of it as such, but in painting farms he was making memorials. His views, in this sense, were of a piece with the pictures of Native Americans that George Catlin, foremost among a number of artists, painted in these decades. It was no secret in the 1830s, when Catlin functioned (courageously) as an itinerant portraitist in terrain west of St. Louis, that Native Americans were being shunted from their lands and that some tribes were on the verge of extinction. A number of years later, Fitz Henry Lane, painting most varieties of sailing ships—his life's work, in effect—presented, though not through conscious design, the beginning of another kind of death spiral: the end of the sailing industry. We periodically get, in his marines, glimpses of death itself, ploughing through the harbors: the steamboat.

Lane, whose father had been a sailmaker and who, because of a lifelong lameness, could not have gone to sea, had, hindsight tells us, an ideal knowledge of, and distance from, his subject. Hicks brought to farming a related sense of intimacy and distance. The idea of farming excited him intellectually and sentimentally. An American of the generation that came to maturity in the years after the new nation got underway, he ascribed to what Hofstadter called the "agrarian myth," which included the belief that the British were vanquished by a "band of embattled farmers." But for Hicks there was another reason to venerate farming life. Such work, he regularly said, bespoke the rudimentary ways by which Jesus and his immediate followers—who formed the egalitarian, priest-free community that Quakers, or certainly Hicks, took as the true exemplars—lived and supported themselves.

His own short career as a farmer, when he was in his mid-thirties, deflated that concept a little. A life in agriculture, he learned, worked better on paper. Farming, he wrote, was a "business which I did not understand." It left him with debts, which drove him to a further round of creditors (and eventually help from Isaac and Samuel Hicks and others). Quick and assured with metaphor, he noted about the circumstances that the "cruel moth of usury was eating up my outward garment."

That thirty years went by before he made a painting of a farm might be because the actual experience of ploughing and planting and tending to animals had been, along with the indebtedness, such a trial for him. That his farm paintings are as strong as they are, on the other hand, may be due to his no longer having to think of farming in an actual, personal way. Working the land for one's immediate needs could be the idea that he originally wanted it to be. And his pictures of the Cornell and Leedom properties may have a special fullness because they weren't even entirely about farming. The subject allowed Hicks to pursue in a different way the issue of a stream, or group, of animals at the bottom of a given scene. The particular and peculiar compositions of these paintings may well have derived from this concern of his.

• • •

It is probably unquestionable that the idea of a procession of animals had to do with death and moving on, perhaps to some deeper connection with the Inner Light. Hicks, it seems, was ready to squeeze out one last aspect of Isaiah's prophesy. This was the prophet's saying, in verse 6, that "a little child shall lead them." This could mean, as it meant in so many of the early Kingdoms, that a child was in charge of the group.

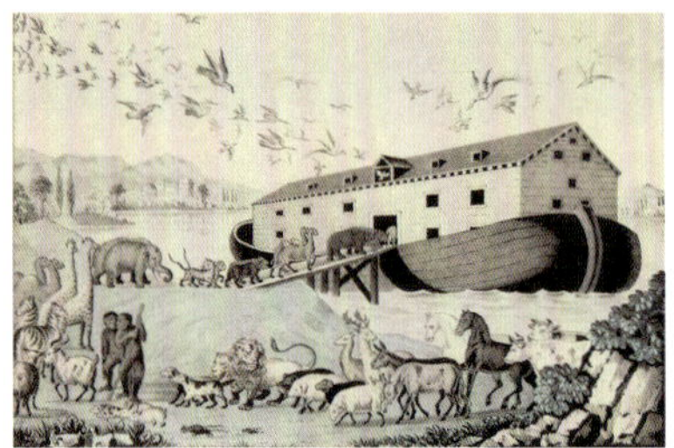

Unknown artist, *Noah's Ark*, 1838–56, 8 1/4 × 12 1/2 in. (21 × 31.8 cm).

But the verb could plausibly suggest that the group, led by the child, goes somewhere. Hicks seems to have adopted this reading.

Conceivably, he got his theme of a procession of animals from the print of Noah's Ark that Currier published in 1844—except that it is not clear if Hicks saw the lithograph that year. What is clear is that, whether or not the print was his inspiration, and regardless of when it came to his attention, he was at this time attracted to the idea, which he would go on and use in any number of his later pictures, of having his characters line up and travel. In 1845, in the Kingdom in the Phillips, he transformed his principals, newly arranged along the bottom of the picture, into what could be a scene of passengers on a platform waiting for a train. After that it wasn't a big leap to make a painting about Noah and his ark, an ultimate story of creatures on the move.

On a quick, first look, it seems as if Hicks no more than copied Currier's print. Then, comparing the painting with the lithograph, it becomes enjoyable to find the changes throughout: the alteration of the land; the deletion of certain couples (monkeys, rats, mice); the addition of others (people, squirrels, rabbits); and so on. Soon, though, the comparatist forgets Currier. It happens because where the print has a bland sky, Hicks created one of the most charged and beautiful skies in nineteenth-century American painting. This is an achievement as the years from the later 1840s into the later 1860s could be called the skyscape period in the nation's art. Sanford Robinson Gifford (whose specialty was a soft atmosphere,

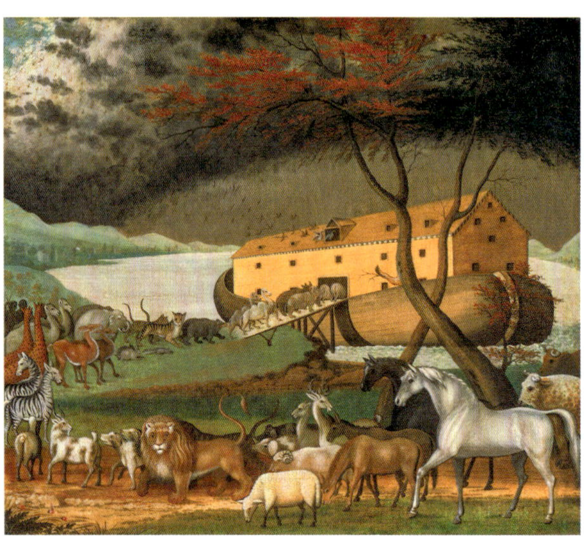

Edward Hicks, *Noah's Ark*, 1846, 26 5/16 × 30 3/8 in. (66.8 × 77.2 cm).

touched with gold and lavender), Frederic Church (who meticulously delineated florid, sunset skies of streaky red, purple, and orange), and Martin Johnson Heade (who was at his best with imminent storm skies of gray and black), were, among others, outdoing one another in the subject.

Hicks's sky is more volatile than those of the younger American painters (and closer to those of his English contemporary John Constable). It has the degrees of darkness that precede a deluge but mixed in with the black clouds are red and green leaves from trees. There is a sunny patch that will soon be obliterated (or may represent life after the flood), and—best of all—countless diving birds, initially hardly visible, seem to be breaking up the storm clouds and propelling them forward simultaneously.

What a sumptuous and muscular handler of color Hicks could be! Look at the picture from a distance and you find the sky's big, curving masses of black and gray interlocking with the big, curving masses of greens and earth colors for the land, the water, and the ark—all forming a layer cake of gently swelling layers going from one side of the scene to the other. Nearly everything expresses the horizontality of the procession of the animals. They face forward as they go, but the male lion—ham of hams—turns to look at us, and way in the distance the young lion, another entertainer, does, too.

Lest the horizontality prove monotonous, two mighty trees provide upright motion. They are not in the original print and are an inspired addition on Hicks's part. They are also a couple (but not one to be saved by Noah). Crossing one another and reaching up to the clouds in identical ways, they seem to be holding back the downpour until the animals get on board. They form a spiritual umbrella. My only qualm with this masterpiece is the glamorous, too-perfect white horse in the corner. She is an instance of Hicks's drawing skill (and heroizing admiration for the animal?) outrunning the style of his picture as a whole.

• • •

HICKS PAINTED HIS *Noah's Ark* in 1846, the year Phebe Ann died and he started his diary. On his sixty-seventh birthday, in April 1847, he thought it was time for "closing my writing concern," and made a final diary entry.

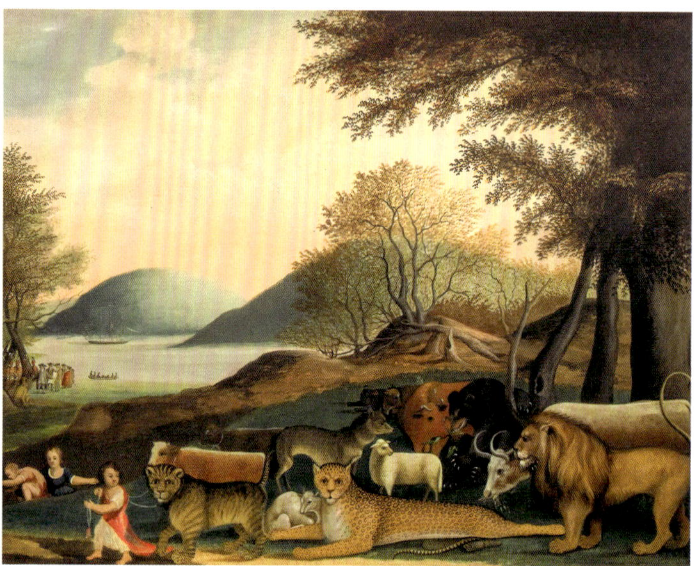

Edward Hicks, *Peaceable Kingdom*, c. 1849, 24 × 30 ¼ in. (60.9 × 76.8).

But then in July 1849, now more certain about his end, he went back to his diary. He wanted to record his feeling for Christ a final time. In his last sentence, he hopes that his faith will prove "a passport from this world to the Heaven of Heavens." But his paintings surely were also passports of a sort. The pictures of his last years suggest that Hicks was living, and preparing to die, through his art.

His last two Kingdoms make this clear. Although they apparently were not made back to back, they could be parts one and two of practically the same moment. They are about departure and have been referred to as such. They show where his many forays into the image of a caravan of creatures placed at the base of a scene had all along been leading.

In the paintings, the child takes on her or his last role. In Kingdoms going back to the early 1830s, this small person had done little more than inconspicuously hold on to the young lion, often in some higher zone toward the back of the scene. In the last Kingdoms, though, the child has a more distinct presence and we believe we look at a girl. She now has a full head of dark hair (after years of a crew cut and then a bald phase) and the appearance of a contemporary child, though dressed in a white toga with a red sash.

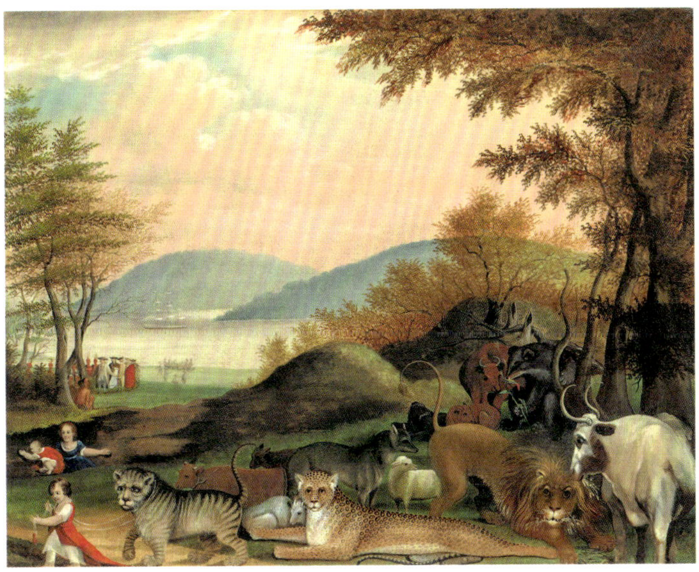

Edward Hicks, *Peaceable Kingdom*, 1849, 24 1⁄4 × 30 1⁄4 in. (61.6 × 76.8 cm).

She has at last tied together all three of her charges—the young lion, the calf, and the fatling—and in Hicks's penultimate Kingdom she and her group are at the head of all the creatures. They are not like the obedient animals that marched off for Noah, but they are at least milling at the bottom edge of the scene. The rope over her shoulder, the child turns her head back to look at them—as if to say "Ready?" The final Kingdom picks up precisely where this one leaves off. Exacting in all his doings, and always aware of timing and his audience, Hicks nearly finished the painting the night before he died. It was made for his daughter Elizabeth, who was probably closer to him than his other children.

In the picture, the child is still at the front of this unregimented group. The lion, in one last burst of individuality, is turned in the wrong direction and appears distracted and feeble, yet mirthful. The ageless beauty, the leopard, is still gauging our response. But the child, the rope over her shoulder, has turned her head forward and is striding forth. A step or two more and she will walk right out of the scene. She is not looking back. She knows they will all surely follow.

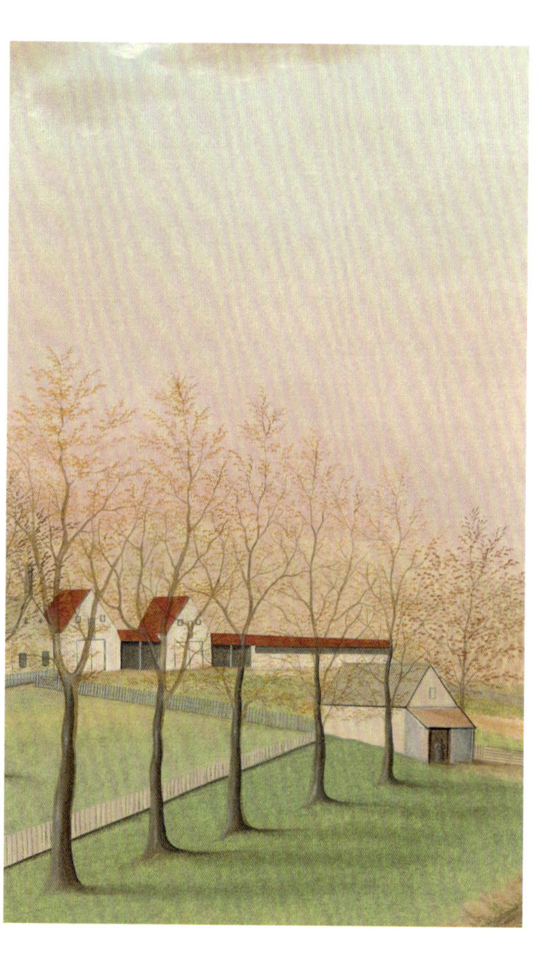

Notes

THE ABBREVIATION in the notes that follow—*EH*—stands for the book entitled *Memoirs of the Life and Religious Labors of Edward Hicks*. It was published in 1851, not long after Hicks's death, and remains available for purchase exactly as it originally appeared through Applewood Books of Bedford, Massachusetts. In this volume, the memoirs are followed with no real break by the diary which Hicks began in February 1846 and kept up to April 1847. It is nearly as long as his memoirs. After his last entry, Hicks returned to his diary one more time, in July 1849, not long before his death.

The Applewood volume contains, as well, two important pieces of writing. The first, "A Little Present for Friends and Friendly People," is the sermon Hicks delivered at Goose Creek, Virginia, in February 1837. Its present form is an amplification of the sermon. The other article in the volume is "A Word of Exhortation to Young Friends," which was originally published in 1845.

In the following notes, a reference to *EH* is usually to the memoirs or the diary, which are similar in tone. If the reference is to the Goose Creek sermon or the address to young Friends, it will be clear in the text which piece of writing is being referred to.

Preface

p. 7 *his funeral*... Noted by Alice Ford, p. 115, in *Edward Hicks: Painter of the Peaceable Kingdom* (1952; reprinted edition 1998) and by Eleanore Price Mather, p. 22, in *Edward Hicks: Primitive Quaker* (1970).

p. 9 *lessons on their mind*... Joan Acocella wrote about Reynard in "Fox News," in the May 4, 2015 *New Yorker*.

An Outdoor Living Room

p. 15 *eroded rims*... Ford makes the only reference that I found to this notable detail of the Kingdoms on p. 4 of her Introduction to the catalogue *Edward Hicks, 1780–1849: A Special Exhibition Devoted to His Life and Work* (1960).

p. 17 *he recalls King Lear*... Seen by Mather on p. 89 of *Edward Hicks: His Peaceable Kingdoms and Other Paintings*, with a text by Mather and a catalogue by Mather and Dorothy Canning Miller (1983).

p. 18 *the lion's superego*... This insight about the ox appears in Mather, as above, on p. 68.

p. 18 *animals whose feelings*... One also thinks of the French illustrator and caricaturist J. J. Grandville, a younger contemporary of Hicks's (he died in 1847, at age forty-three), whose delectable lithographic fantasies present the world of the Paris of this time as populated, in many of his best known images, by cats, dogs, pigs, an assembly of insects, and so on. Their fashion sense is highly developed.

A Late Beginning

p. 21 *Christian religiosity*... For Wood's pronouncement on the American religious revival, see *The New York Review of Books*, July 9, 2015, p. 27.

p. 21 *popular art form*... Matthiessen's judgment about the public lecture in antebellum America appears in his *American Renaissance: Art and Expression in the Age of Emerson and Whitman* (1941), on p. 551.

p. 21 *unsparing tongue*... Edward's truth-telling nature is noted by Alice Ford in her *Edward Hicks: Painter of the Peaceable Kingdom* (1952; reprinted edition 1998), on p. 104.

p. 21 *Quakers who were artists*... The thorny issues of being a Quaker and an artist, and Quaker aesthetics, are gone into by Eleanore Price Mather, particularly pp. 49 to 53 of *Edward Hicks: His Peaceable Kingdoms and Other Paintings*, with a text by Mather and a catalogue by Mather and Dorothy Canning Miller (1983).

p. 21 *a fine artist*... Hicks sees the very idea of art for its own sake as an affront on p. 71 of *EH*.

p. 22 *borrowed freely*... Cahill makes a strong case for borrowing on p. 9 of *American Folk Art: The Art of the Common Man in America, 1750–1900* (1932).

p. 23 *self-trained artist*... Eitner's comment on artistic learning appears on the first page of his introduction to an unpaginated 1987 Géricault exhibition held at the Salander-O'Reilly Gallery, New York City.

p. 24 *archetypal folk artist*... Mary Black, in *American Naive Paintings from the National Gal-*

lery of Art (1985), writes definitively on p. 15, "Perhaps the best-known, but in some ways least-typical, of American folk painters was Edward Hicks."

p. 24 *uncommonly dogmatical* . . . Edward, in *EH*, p. 53, catches a key component of his nature.

p. 24 *hotly defended himself* . . . Hicks is nearly wrecked by his strong-armed defensiveness on p. 61 of *EH*.

p. 24 *fund of nonsense* . . . The reader wishes Edward had said more about his comic side, here noted in *EH*, p. 34.

p. 24 *a born entertainer* . . . Always digging beneath the obvious interpretation, Mather found, I think brilliantly—in *Edward Hicks: Primitive Quaker* (Pendle Hill Pamphlet 170, 1970), p. 7—a way to characterize Hicks that seems not to have occurred to any other commentator.

p. 24 *straitened* . . . Edward sees the tight situations he always gets in on p. 146 of *EH* and is troubled by his loquacity on p. 174.

p. 24 *zig-zag nature* . . . Edward confesses his extreme inconsistency on p. 214 of *EH*, sees the traps he can fall into as a minister on p. 151, and is torn by the tensions of everyday life on p. 146.

p. 26 *humble industry* . . . Hicks often refers to the "humble industry" of the first Christians—see p. 65 and p. 121 of *EH* for examples—and Ford, as above, looks into the ambiguities of the idea for Hicks on her pp. 27, 28.

p. 26 *he grew wheat* . . . Hicks's farming experience is detailed on p. 204 of Edna S. Pullinger's "Edward Hicks, Newtown Coach Painter, among Friends," *Bucks County Historical Society Journal*, II (1979).

p. 26 *orders for decorating* . . . What Hicks ornamented is gone into in Ford, as above, p. 22, and Pullinger, as above, p. 214.

p. 26 *Martin Johnson Heade* . . . In his 1999 *Martin Johnson Heade*, Theodore E. Stebbins, Jr., our foremost authority on the subject, notes on p. 1 that Heade, who was born in Bucks County in 1819 and left in 1842, "learned the rudiments of his craft" from Hicks, and Stebbins calls Heade on p. 169 an "apprentice" to the Newtown painter.

p. 27 *especially alive* . . . See Ford, as above, p. 6, for General Washington's visit to Newtown.

p. 27 *small, book-length poem* . . . Hicks would have known that, as Edna S. Pullinger writes on p. 12 of her *Newtown's First Library Building* (1976), *The Foresters* was initially published in book form by Asher Miner's Press in Newtown. It is currently available as a paperback from Forgotten Books.

p. 28 *has been called* . . . Mather (1970), as above, p. 10, writes that *Noah's Ark* is "perhaps the most beautiful of his works."

p. 29 *American Romanticism* . . . Tatham sees the need for Hicks to be viewed in the wider culture of the nineteenth century in his "Edward Hicks, Elias Hicks and John Comly: Perspectives on the Peaceable Kingdom Theme," *American Art Journal*, XIII (1981), pp. 37, 41, 50.

p. 31 *in moods of pessimism* . . . Chase's thought about what can be called agrarian, Romantic, or antebellum America is on p. 15 of his Whitman study.

p. 35 *a fair of antiques* . . . Ford, as above, writes about the Bucks County Bi-Centennial Celebration, held in Doylestown, on p. 83 and p. 121.

p. 36 *has been said* . . . Stillinger links awareness of folk-art forms with the new art of the late nineteenth and early twentieth centuries on p. 145 of her *A Kind of Archeology: Collecting American Folk Art, 1876–1976* (2011), and she emphasizes the roles that Holger Cahill, Edith Halpert, and Abby Aldrich Rockefeller played in fostering this awareness on pp. 218–53.

p. 37 *people had collected it before* . . . The Nadelmans' involvement in what they called folk and peasant arts is rendered in great detail in *Making It Modern: The Folk Art Collection of Elie and Viola Nadelman* (2015).

p. 37 *the museum's collection* . . . For the subsequent homes of this painting, now in the Abby Aldrich Rockefeller Folk Art Museum in Colonial Williamsburg, see Mather and Miller, as above, p. 194. Mrs. Rockefeller ultimately bought four paintings by Hicks and the Museum added twelve more in later years.

p. 37 *Léger's views* . . . The French painter's feeling for Hicks appears in *The Art Digest*, December 15, 1931, p. 13.

p. 38 *very words peaceable kingdom* . . . That the words peaceable kingdom derive from the Westhall illustration, see Ford, as above, p. 42.

p. 38 *convincingly writes* . . . This statement on folk-art trailblazers appears on p. 218 of Stillinger, as above.

p. 38 *on first sight* . . . Carlen notes his feelings about Hicks in an Oral history interview with Catherine Stover, done in 1985, on file at the Archives of American Art. His gallery on 16th Street was in the house he and his family lived in, meaning that the Quaker painter became over the years practically a member of the family. His daughter Nancy remembered "being wakened in the middle of the night every time father came home with another Hicks. We would all stand around staring at it."

p. 38 *in Bucks County* . . . Ford talks about Carlen's intentions and her own expectations in a letter, in the Robert Carlen papers in the Archives of American Art, dated April 24, 1950.

p. 39 *trying to quell* . . . Held's article, "Edward Hicks and the Tradition," appears in *Art Quarterly*, XIV (1951), pp. 121–56.

p. 39 *very rare illustrations* . . . Held, as above, p. 130, notes the rarity of Isaiah's prophesy in art.

p. 40 *a lifelong dream* . . . Gordon refers to her acquisition of a *Peaceable Kingdom* on p. 11 of *A Shared Legacy: Folk Art in America* (2014).

p. 40 *two panoramically wide* . . . Huge's *Composite Harbor Scene with Castle*, c. 1875, is in the National Gallery of Art and his *Composite Harbor Scene with Volcano* is in the de Young Museum, San Francisco.

p. 41 *outsider artists* . . . The term first appeared as the title of Roger Cardinal's *Outsider Art* (1972); and recent exhibition catalogues that deal with the different terms and give a sense of the scope of this art include *"Great and Mighty Things": Outsider Art from the Jill and Sheldon Bonovitz Collection* (2013) and *Outliers and American Vanguard Art* (2018).

p. 43 *all over Newtown* . . . Hicks's active involvement in the town's life, and a look at the staggering amount of work he took on, can be found in Pullinger, as above.

p. 43 *fairly prosperous* . . . Black, as above, refers to the social status of folk painters on p. 9 and their allure for professional artists on p. 17.

p. 45 *little-tutored and self-taught* . . . Black, as above, p. 8, uses these adjectives to describe naive or folk artists.

p. 47 *full museum retrospective* . . . It was *Thomas Chambers: American Marine and Landscape Painter, 1808–1869* (2008), organized by Kathleen A. Forster, who also wrote its catalogue.

p. 49 *organic growth* . . . Tatham, as above, p. 40, sees the development in Hicks's pictures.

p. 50 *looming giants* . . . In *Erastus Salisbury Field: 1805–1900* (1984), Mary Black refers to the largeness of the figures on p. 34 and their bearing on p. 28.

p. 51 *so labored and absurd* . . . See Richardson's *Painting in America: From 1502 to the Present* (1956), p. 211, for these words on Field.

p. 53 *unusually warm weather* . . . Mr. Shoener's comment appears in Andy Newman's "Unseasonable Greetings in a New York Searching for Jack Frost," *The New York Times*, December 23, 2015, p. 18.

p. 54 *become leaders* . . . Hicks's statement is found in *EH*, p. 321 (where he includes a comma after "people" and "be").

The Families

p. 56 *edified and encouraged* . . . Hicks talks about Penn's sermons on p. 147 of *EH*.

p. 57 *must tremble* . . . The origin of the word "Quaker" appears on p. 3 of William J. Whalen's *The Quakers or Our Neighbors, The Friends* (1982).

p. 58 *Zen meditation* . . . Howard H. Brinton looks at the meeting for worship on pp. 102, 103 of his *Friends for 350 Years*, with historical update by Margaret Hope Bacon (1952; revised 2002). Much of my understanding of the Society of Friends comes from Brinton's book.

p. 58 *little difference* . . . I have drawn this reading of the Inner Light from Brinton, as above, p. 54.

p. 59 *superior women* . . . Edward pronounces on some women on p. 136 of *EH*.

p. 59 *the stately dramatic* . . . Melville characterizes Quaker idiom on p. 107 of the Modern Library edition of *Moby-Dick* (1930).

p. 60 *an explicit purpose* . . . Whitehead's statement appears in his 1933 *Adventures in Ideas* and is quoted by Edwin H. Cady in his *John Woolman: The Mind of the Quaker Saint* (1966) on p. 169.

p. 60 *an international clearinghouse* . . . Wills writes about Quakers on pp. 135–52 of his 2007 *Head and Heart*. The book's dedication reads "*To Anthony Benezet* AMERICAN SAINT."

p. 61 *ready to pounce* . . . Edward's vigilance in regard to his fellow ministers is found in *EH*, p. 105.

p. 61 *his own sermons* . . . About records made of sermons, see p. 43 of *Edward Hicks: His Peaceable Kingdoms and Other Paintings* (1983), text by Eleanore Price Mather and catalogue by Dorothy Canning Miller and Eleanore Price Mather.

p. 62 *the contingent expenses* . . . Edward describes his ministerial duties on p. 225 of *EH*.

p. 62 *she suddenly wondered* . . . Kennedy's words on the St. Louis scene appear on p. 63 of Alice Ford's *Edward Hicks: Painter of the Peaceable Kingdom* (1952; reprinted edition 1998).

p. 62 *searching and lively* . . . Elias's comment on Edward's preaching is quoted by Ford, as above, p. 39.

p. 63 *Isaac had turned*... The importance of the New York-based Isaac Hicks is addressed by Bliss Forbush on p. 130 of his *Elias Hicks: Quaker Liberal* (1956).

p. 63 *came to Edward's aid*... Alice Ford describes the role of Henry Hicks (and that of other family members and friends) in publishing Edward's *Memoirs* in her "The Publication of Edward Hicks's *Memoirs*," which appeared in the *Bulletin of Friends Historical Association*, 50 (Spring 1961), pp. 4–11.

p. 63 *main problem of Quakerism*... Heard's quote, taken from his 1939 *A Quaker Mutation*, appears on p. 75 of Mather's 1980 history of Pendle Hill, the Quaker center outside Philadelphia.

p. 64 *color more nebulous*... Mather, as above, handles the "drab" issue on p. 53.

p. 64 *drab-colored eye*... Melville, as above, notes Captain Bildad's different drabnesses on p. 109.

p. 64 *when they come*... Lamb's thoughts and observations on Quakers are from his 1821 "A Quakers' Meeting." It appears in *Charles Lamb: Selected Prose* (1985), edited by Adam Phillips, and both quotes are from its p. 104.

p. 65 *well-to-do family*... The status and relative wealth of the Hicks family are noted in many places in Ford, as above—see pp. 5, 7 and p. 27 for examples.

p. 66 *found himself a home*... Edward describes his catching the attention of Elizabeth Twining on p. 21 of *EH*.

p. 66 *gentleman's son*... Edward so describes his Twining family upbringing on p. 34 of *EH*.

p. 66 *Beulah*... About Beulah Twining, see *EH*, p. 23.

p. 67 *not having the aptitude*... The reader will find in *EH*, pp. 25, 26, and 33, a number of instances where, according to Edward, Isaac expressed his disappointment in his second son.

p. 67 *unable to understand*... Edna S. Pullinger goes into detail on Isaac and the grown Edward on pp. 8, 9 of her *Newtown's First Library Building* (1976).

p. 68 *Dr. Gilbert Hicks*... On p. 26 of *EH*, Edward salutes his brother, who became "a humble practical Christian."

p. 68 *primitive Christianity*... Hicks's sense of Quakerism's purpose comes on p. 96 of *EH*.

p. 68 *first Christians*... Alice Ford, as above, goes into the allure of the early Christians and humble industry on p. 27.

p. 69 *truth inwardly known*... Cady, as above, touches on Quaker anti-intellectualism on p. 41.

p. 69 *democratic model*... Hicks refers to the revolutionary nature of the Society on p. 120 of *EH* and to the republican tenor of Christ and his fellowship on p. 97.

p. 69 *letters from his mother*... About the letters see Ford, as above, p. 117 and Mather, as above, p. 81.

p. 69 *called love letters*... By Ford, as above, p. 28, and she quotes the two of them on p. 117.

p. 70 *wanted to believe*... Edward's sense of his mother's last awarenesses can be found on p. 20 of *EH*.

p. 70 *even forbidding*... Isaac's stern demeanor is noted by Ford, as above, on p. 13 and numerous other places.

p. 70 *town library*... Information on this subject can be found in Pullinger, as above, who also describes Hicks's tastes in poetry and his particular love for Alexander Wilson's *The Foresters*.

p. 70 *striking words* . . . Isaac's letter seeking help is found in Ford, as above, p. 14.

p. 71 *softened version* . . . Weekley draws attention to the editing of Hicks's *Memoirs* in her *The Kingdoms of Edward Hicks* (with the assistance of Laura Pass Barry; 1999), pp. xiv, xv. Ford offers her different opinion on p. 108 of her biography of the painter, as above. On p. 11 of her *Bulletin* article on the subject, as above, she adds that, while the *Memoirs* is fully Edward's work, his actual manuscript was "discarded" when Oliver Hough, the scrivener, made the copy for the publisher.

p. 72 *scattered, shattered* . . . Edward's adjectives are on p. 191 of *EH*.

p. 72 *a J. M.* . . . Comments about fellow preachers appear on p. 202 of *EH*.

p. 72 *crisp* . . . Mather, as above, on p. 72, so describes Hicks's estimates of his contemporaries.

p. 72 *became a carouser* . . . For Edward's reprobate past, see *EH*, pp. 37–39.

p. 73 *this sanguine cheer* . . . Hicks describes this difficult time for him on pp. 36, 37, and 40 of *EH*.

p. 73 *denounced every one* . . . Edward's vituperative and castigating nature is on display in *EH* on p. 51.

p. 73 *two or three weeks* . . . Hicks describes his first speaking in meeting on p. 54 of *EH* and passes judgment on a hypocrite on p. 80.

p. 73 *my sermon* . . . Hicks denigrates his sermon while showing the Methodist minister as a ninny at the same time on p. 81 of *EH;* and sees Quaker ministers as subject to becoming swellheaded as any other kind of minister on p. 152.

p. 74 *when Friends give way* . . . The obsessions of Friends gone into in *EH*, pp. 121, 122.

p. 74 *choleric, turbulent* . . . Hicks sees himself as mannerless and superior on p. 100 of *EH;* notes his having enemies on p. 130; and slams a detractor on pp. 130, 131.

p. 74 *hireling* . . . Wills, as above, refers to Milton's designation on p. 138. One sees as well "hireling priest" and "hireling priesthood." Hicks puts his spin on the professional ecclesiastic on p. 134 of *EH*. On p. 123 he amusingly ridicules priestly education.

p. 74 *gentlemen dentists* . . . A term of reproach that appears in *EH*, p. 64, and that may be original to Hicks.

p. 74 *a deathbed scene* . . . This farcical conjecture appears in *EH* on p. 114.

p. 75 *playing out again* . . . A link between the Quaker rift and the American Revolution made by Hicks in *EH*, p. 110.

p. 75 *unsuited for* . . . Forbush, as above, looks at quietism on p. 55.

p. 76 *Whitman's grandfather* . . . Forbush, as above, p. 9, notes a connection with Elias.

p. 76 *proposal to boycott* . . . Elias's plan is referred to by Forbush, as above, pp. 89, 90.

p. 77 *Elias addressed Baptists* . . . For his fearlessness, see Forbush, as above, p. 77.

p. 77 *the state house* . . . Bliss Forbush, as above, refers to Elias's speaking at different state houses and before audiences including governors on pp. 161, 162, 230.

p. 77 *Whitman remembered* . . . Whitman's memory of hearing Elias is noted by Forbush, as above, on p. 163, and the ballroom scene is described by Kaplan in his *Walt Whitman: A Life* (1980), p. 68.

p. 77 *many guests* . . . From a list of sentences taken from Elias's sermons by Forbush, as above, p. 166—sentences that Forbush rightly says would have "lingered" with Elias's listeners.

p. 77 *faster than* . . . Elias's words, from 1829, are quoted by Forbush, as above, on p. 279.

p. 78 *carefully to wait*... Elias's admonition to seek an emptying out of one's self appears on p. 56 of Forbush, as above.

p. 78 *uniformity of belief*... Elias's conviction that a creed-based religion is ultimately irreligious can be found on p. 216 of Forbush, as above, and his openness to faiths other than Christianity appears on Forbush's p. 224.

p. 78 *more kinship*... Emerson's closeness to Quaker thinking is found on p. 9 of Mathiessen's *American Renaissance: Art and Expression in the Age of Emerson and Whitman* (1941).

p. 79 *supercilious and insulting*... Hicks describes Orthodox ministers at their worst on pp. 126, 127 of *EH*.

p. 79 *Royal Americans*... Edward lambastes the Orthodox with a choice epithet in *EH* on p. 124.

p. 80 *the primitive spirit*... Lamb's uncertainty as to where the Quakers were going appears on p. 102 in Phillips's selection, as above.

p. 80 *nearest and dearest*... Edward describes how harmful the Orthodox were in *EH* on p. 106 and pp. 97, 98.

p. 80 *in a letter*... Edward's 1840 letter to Hugh can be found in the Hicks papers of the Friends Historical Society.

p. 80 *meant disparagingly*... Tatham notes how the names behind the Quaker schism came about in "Edward Hicks, Elias Hicks and John Comly: Perspectives on the Peaceable Kingdoms Theme," *American Art Journal*, XIII (1981), p. 41, n. 12.

p. 80 *flushed with victory*... Hicks's reports from the front lines are from *EH*, p. 104 and pp. 124, 125.

p. 81 *altogether less substance*... Forbush, as above, writes on p. 248 that "Elias could hardly believe that all the stir and confusion among Friends was the result of 'a little difference of opinion on abstract subjects'... 'How can we ask or hope for better days,' he exclaimed, 'until the greatly oppressed is redressed and relieved from cruel bondage.' "

The Kingdoms

p. 82 *malignant and bitter*... Hicks describes Evans on p. 138 of *EH*.

p. 82 *offended him*... See p. 185 of *EH* where Hicks says he is glad he didn't offend a friend.

p. 83 *Quaker thinking*... How the Kingdoms exemplified Quaker thought can be found on p. 19 of *Edward Hicks: His Peaceable Kingdoms and Other Paintings*, text by Eleanore Price Mather and catalogue by Mather and Dorothy Canning Miller (1983) and on p. 92 of *The Kingdoms of Edward Hicks* by Carolyn Weekley (with the assistance of Laura Pass Barry; 1999).

p. 83 *spoke positively about art*... The incident is referred to in Mather, as above, p. 51, and in Alice Ford, *Edward Hicks: Painter of the Peaceable Kingdom* (1952; reprinted 1998), p. 122.

p. 84 *value to the community*... On p. 33, Weekley, as above, writes that the elders might have countenanced Hicks's being a painter because of his work as a minister.

p. 84 *exhibitions*... References to Hicks and his family and art shows can be found in Ford, as above, p. 43.

p. 84 *fondness for painting* . . . Hicks says that his feeling for painting keeps him from being a model Friend in *EH* on p. 12.

p. 85 *insignificant painter* . . . Hicks identifies himself as a painter because of his way of embellishing stories on p. 72 of *EH*, and sees himself as simply a mere painter on p. 149.

p. 85 *trifling, insignificant arts* . . . Hicks so labels painting in *EH*, p. 71.

p. 85 *they were popular* . . . Ford, as above, p. 91, describes, fleetingly, the audience for Hicks's pictures.

p. 85 *to raise money* . . . Ford, as above, p. 88, quotes the letter to Hart in which Hicks describes in detail how little the pictures matter to him, saying in different ways "I don't care much about them."

p. 86 *or burn them* . . . For the Luis Jones letter, see Ford, as above, pp. 81, 82.

p. 87 *a real creative effort* . . . Held's verdict appears on p. 133 of his "Edward Hicks and the Tradition," *Art Quarterly* XIV (1951).

p. 87 *a copyist* . . . Ford calls Hicks "primarily a copyist" on pp. 43, 44, as above; but she also writes on p. 108 about Hicks's 1848 painting of the Cornell farm—about which, to "not a few," it is his "outstanding work"—that it is "his answer to those who would today call him a mere copyist."

p. 88 *collages* . . . Ford so describes the Kingdoms on p. 42, as above.

p. 91 *playing with the Scriptural* . . . Tatham makes this point on pp. 44, 45 of his "Edward Hicks, Elias Hicks and John Comly: Perspectives on the Peaceable Kingdom Theme," *American Art Journal* XIII (1981).

p. 93 *remain little known* . . . many of Wilson's drawings can be found in the authoritative *Alexander Wilson: The Scot Who Founded American Ornithology*, by Edward H. Burtt, Jr. and William E. Davis, Jr. (2013).

p. 94 *growing local interest* . . . Pullinger notes this new taste for classical art on p. 50 of her 1973 *A Dream of Peace: Edward Hicks of Newtown*.

p. 94 *foretell a Christian future* . . . Mather, as above, delves on p. 19 into the prophetic nature of the child and of Isaiah, pointing out that his words foretell for Christians even the birth of Christ (which is why in scenes of the Annunciation the book Mary is reading is turned to Isaiah).

p. 95 *waste places* . . . Edward's powerful words aimed at young Quakers are in *EH*, p. 337.

p. 95 *he saw missionary travel* . . . Edward's revised thoughts on missionary travel appear in *EH*, pp. 352–355.

p. 95 *fanatical melancholy* . . . This funny passage on missionaries is on p. 355 of *EH*.

p. 95 *saving the Society* . . . Hicks exhorts his young audience on p. 343 of *EH*.

p. 96 *no sexes in souls* . . . This pronouncement appears in *EH* on p. 293.

p. 98 *to do with Elias* . . . Tatham, as above, proposes Elias as the reason for Edward's continued painting on pp. 45, 46.

p. 98 *in the first place* . . . Tatham speculates on p. 46, n. 23, as above, that it was Elias who gave Edward the idea of painting the prophesy to begin with.

p. 99 *a willful avoidance* . . . Tatham's suggestion that Hicks the painter avoided sophistication is on his p. 39, as above.

p. 101 *wild and not tame* . . . Richardson, in his monumental *Emerson: The Mind on Fire* (1995), extrapolates his subject's thought beginning on p. 272, and on the same page Richardson writes that the "main point" of this same lecture of Emerson's is "the Quaker one that the inner light or the still small voice is not whim or personal preference but a person's own and only window on the real light, the molten core, the one deep well of life."

p. 101 *a wide field* . . . Edward characterizes his Goose Creek sermon on p. 267 of *EH*.

p. 101 *Isaiah's prophesy* . . . Hicks begins to set out his reading of Isaiah and a connection between the carnivorous animals and the four temperaments on p. 268 and on p. 270 of *EH*.

p. 102 *the temperaments* . . . Mather, p. 69, as above, says we do not know how Hicks "acquired these fragments of late classical and medieval lore" and that he mentioned the subject already in 1827.

p. 102 *principal elements* . . . Hicks sets out the elements on p. 268 of *EH*.

p. 102 *under cover* . . . See *EH*, p. 276, for these notes on the wolf.

p. 103 *melancholics hide* . . . Hicks links the issues of melancholics and duplicity on pp. 276, 277 of *EH*.

p. 103 *most suicides* . . . Hicks characterizes Judas and John in *EH*, p. 282.

p. 105 *figure of unreliability* . . . These words on the leopard appear in *EH* on p. 287.

p. 105 *changeable and chaffy* . . . Edward uses this word on p. 290 of *EH*.

p. 106 *the leopard screams* . . . The sounds of the carnivores are found on p. 288 of *EH*.

p. 107 *more imagination* . . . These descriptions of the sanguine are in *EH* on p. 290.

p. 107 *the sanguine find* . . . Hicks describes the sanguine spirit on p. 291 of *EH*.

p. 107 *it has few leopards* . . . Mather, as above, p. 68, distinguishes among Quakers.

p. 107 *dull and inert* . . . See p. 307 of *EH* for Hicks on the phlegmatic.

p. 108 *a proud, power-hungry* . . . These words on the lion are from *EH*, pp. 321, 322.

p. 108 *Saint Paul* . . . On p. 326 of *EH*, Hicks notes Paul's temperament.

p. 109 *riven by the guilt* . . . Mather, as above, p. 47, describes this phase of the lion's development.

p. 109 *a tenuous peace* . . . These tense Kingdoms are described by Weekley, as above, on p. 123.

p. 110 *clown among lions* . . . Mather, as above, zeroes in on the Brooklyn lion on p. 47.

p. 110 *the most sophisticated* . . . This judgment on the Kingdoms appears on p. 123 of Weekley, as above.

An Open Door

p. 113 *particular friends* . . . Hicks begins noting the deaths of people close to him on p. 139 of *EH*.

p. 113 *invited to the funeral* . . . The invitation is noted on p. 230 of *EH*.

p. 114 *was buried last week* . . . These references to deaths and funerals appear in *EH* on pp. 139–51.

p. 114 *speak at funerals* . . . See *EH*, pp. 152, 153, for these further references to funerals and p. 157 for the invitation to speak at Wrightstown.

p. 115 *a mere shadow* . . . Hicks writes about Hannah Parker in *EH* on pp. 166–69.

p. 115 *my serious thoughtfulness* . . . These words about his mortality are found in *EH*, p. 153.

p. 115 *much snow* . . . Edward touches on the weather on p. 140 of *EH*.

p. 115 *my favorite* . . . Phebe Ann's importance noted in *EH* on p. 159.

p. 115 *most intense suffering* . . . These references to the family's loss are on p. 142 of *EH*.

p. 116 *a long letter* . . . Phebe Ann's letter is quoted by Alice Ford in her *Edward Hicks: Painter of the Peaceable Kingdom* (1952; reprinted 1998), p. 99.

p. 116 *a singular thing* . . . Edward's missing the funeral appears in *EH* on p. 152.

p. 119 *which he never saw* . . . What print source Hicks used for his paintings of William Penn's grave, and why he in all likelihood was unaware of H. F. de Cort's original oil of the subject, which was in the Historical Society of Pennsylvania, is gone into by Ford, as above, on p. 105.

p. 122 *pigs at a trough* . . . Eleanore Price Mather characterizes their tails on p. 14 of her *Edward Hicks: Primitive Quaker* (1970).

p. 122 *the word contentment* . . . Flexner's word on Durrie appears on p. 256 of his *That Wilder Image* (1962).

p. 126 *commercial farming* . . . Hofstadter describes the demise of the yeoman farmer and the transformation of American agriculture on pp. 23–59 of his *The Age of Reform: From Bryan to F. D. R.* (1955), and notes the situation in Ohio on p. 39.

p. 127 *career as a farmer* . . . Hicks's comments about his farming days and his ensuing debts can be found in *EH*, p. 71.

p. 130 *a passport* . . . These last words of Hicks's diary appear on p. 261 of *EH*.

Image Credits

p. 6 Edward Hicks, *Peaceable Kingdom* (1845–46), oil on canvas, 24 1⁄8 × 32 1⁄8 in. (61.3 × 81.6 cm), detail. The Phillips Collection, Washington, DC; acquired 1939.

p. 10 Edward Hicks, *Peaceable Kingdom* (c. 1830–32), oil on canvas, 17 7⁄8 × 23 7⁄8 in. (45.5 × 60.6 cm). The Metropolitan Museum of Art, New York, NY; gift of Edgar William and Bernice Chrysler Garbisch, 1970. © The Metropolitan Museum of Art. Courtesy Art Resource, NY.

p. 12 Horace Pippin, *The Holy Mountain III* (1945), oil on canvas, 25 1⁄4 × 30 1⁄4 in. (64.6 × 76.8 cm). Hirshhorn Museum and Sculpture Garden, Washington, DC; gift of Joseph H. Hirshhorn, 1966. Photo: Cathy Carver.

p. 13 Sharon Horvath, *Peaceable (for Edward Hicks)* (2008), pigment, polymer, and ink on paper mounted on canvas, 52 × 48 in. (132 × 122 cm). Private collection. Photo courtesy The Drawing Room, East Hampton, NY.

p. 15 Pisanello, *The Vision of Saint Eustace* (c. 1438–42), egg tempera on wood, 21 1⁄2 × 25 3⁄4 in. (54.8 × 65.5 cm). National Gallery, London; purchased 1895. © The National Gallery, London.

p. 16 Edward Hicks, *Peaceable Kingdom* (1846–47), oil on canvas, 26 × 32 1⁄2 in. (64.5 × 82.5 cm). Private collection. Courtesy Sotheby's, Inc. © 2020.

p. 17 Edward Hicks, *Peaceable Kingdom* (c. 1833), oil on canvas, 17 7⁄8 × 23 15⁄16 in. (45.4 × 60.8 cm). Pennsylvania Academy of the Fine Arts, Philadelphia, PA; John S. Phillips bequest, by exchange (acquired from the Philadelphia Museum of Art, originally the 1950 bequest of Lisa Norris Elkins).

p. 17 Edward Hicks, *Peaceable Kingdom* (c. 1849), oil on canvas, 24 × 30 1⁄4 in. (60.9 × 76.8), detail. Private collection. Courtesy Galerie St. Etienne, New York.

p. 18 George Herriman, *Ignatz Mouse, Officer Pupp, and Krazy Kat*, watercolor sent to a fan (c. 1925). Private collection.

p. 27 Edward Hicks, *The Falls of Niagara* (c. 1825), oil on canvas, 31 1⁄2 × 38 in. (80 × 96.5 cm). The Metropolitan Museum of Art, New York, NY; gift of Edgar William and Bernice Chrysler Garbisch, 1962.

p. 28 Edward Hicks, *The Residence of David Twining* (c. 1845–46), oil on canvas, 26 × 29 1/2 in. (66 × 74.9 cm). Carnegie Museum of Art, Pittsburgh, PA; Howard N. Eavenson Memorial Fund for the Howard N. Eavenson Americana Collection, 62.39.

p. 31 Alexander Wilson, *Rough-legged Hawk*. Ernst Mayr Library, Museum of Comparative Zoology, Harvard University, Cambridge, MA.

p. 31 George Catlin, *Shón-ka-ki-he-ga, Horse Chief, Grand Pawnee Head Chief* (1832), oil on canvas, 29 × 24 in. (73.7 × 60.9 cm). Smithsonian American Art Museum, Washington, DC; gift of Mrs. Joseph Harrison, Jr.

p. 33 Richard Caton Woodville, *Politics in an Oyster House* (1848), 16 1/4 × 13 1/16 in. (41.2 × 33.1 cm). The Walters Art Museum, Baltimore, MD; gift of C. Morgan Marshall, 1945.

p. 34 William Sidney Mount, *After Dinner* (1834), oil on wood, 10 7/8 × 10 15/16 in. (27.6 × 27.8 cm). Yale University Art Gallery, New Haven, CT.

p. 34 Charles Deas, *The Death Struggle* (1840–45), oil on canvas, 30 × 25 in. (76.2 × 63.5 cm). Shelburne Museum, Shelburne, VT; museum purchase, acquired from Maxim Karolik, 1959-265.16. Photo: Bruce Schwarz.

p. 37 Edward Hicks, *Peaceable Kingdom* (c. 1833), oil on canvas, 17 1/2 × 23 11/16 in. (44.5 × 60.2 cm). Worcester Art Museum, Worcester, MA. Courtesy Bridgeman Images.

p. 40 Edward Hicks, *Peaceable Kingdom* (1835–40), oil on canvas, 26 × 29 1/2 in. (66 × 74.9 cm). Private collection. Courtesy Christie's Images / Bridgeman Images.

p. 41 Adolf Wölfli, *Rhodanus, Spain* (1910), *From the Cradle to the Grave*, book 4, p. 159, pencil and colored pencil on newsprint, 39 1/4 × 28 1/4 in. (99.7 × 71.7 cm). Kunstmuseum Bern, A9243-16.

p. 42 Martín Ramírez, *Untitled* (1954), graphite, colored pencil, watercolor, and crayon on paper, 52 3/16 × 23 15/16 in. (132.6 × 60.8 cm). Solomon R. Guggenheim Museum, New York; gift of the Estate of Martin Ramirez, 2008. © Estate of Martín Ramírez. Courtesy The Solomon R. Guggenheim Foundation / Art Resource, NY.

p. 44 Edward Hicks, *Penn's Treaty with the Indians* (1840–45), oil on canvas, 25 × 30 1/4 in. (63.5 × 76.8 cm). Shelburne Museum, Shelburne, VT; museum purchase, acquired from Edith Halpert, The Downtown Gallery, 1953-1179. Photo: Bruce Schwarz.

p. 45 Edward Hicks, *Washington Crossing the Delaware* (1833), oil on canvas originally mounted on wood panel, 31 1/2 × 31 1/2 in. (80 × 80 cm). Mercer Museum of the Bucks County Historical Society, Doylestown, PA.

p. 46 George S. Lang, *Washington Passing the Delaware*, engraving after a painting by Thomas Sully, etched by William Humphrys, published by Samuel Augustus Mitchell, Philadelphia, May 20, 1825 (printed by B. Rogers). Library of Congress Prints and Photographs Division, Washington, DC.

p. 47 Ammi Phillips, *Girl in a Red Dress with Cat and Dog* (1830–35), oil on canvas, 30 × 25 in. (76.2 × 63.5 cm). American Folk Art Museum, New York, NY; gift of Ralph Esmerian, 2001.37.1. Courtesy American Folk Art Museum / Art Resource, NY.

p. 47 Jacob Maentel, *Dr. Christian Bucher* (c. 1825-1830), watercolor, gouache, ink, and pencil on paper, 16 1/2 × 10 1/2 in. (41.9 × 26.7 cm), American Folk Art Museum, New York, NY, Gift of Ralph Esmerian. 2013.1.8. Courtesy American Folk Art Museum / Art Resource, NY.

p. 48 Thomas Chambers, *View of Cold Spring and Mount Taurus from Fort Putnam* (1845–55), oil on canvas, 42 5⁄8 × 58 in. (108.4 × 147.3 cm). Fenimore Art Museum, Cooperstown, NY; museum purchase, N0011.1999. Photo: Richard Walker.

p. 49 James Bard, *The Steamboat "Isaac Smith" on the Hudson River* (1861), oil on canvas, 31 × 52 in. (78.7 × 132 cm). Private collection. Photo: Andrew Davis; courtesy Bourgeault-Horan Auctions.

p. 50 Erastus Salisbury Field, *Charles Backus Jones* (c. 1833), oil on canvas, 35 7⁄16 × 29 7⁄16 in. (90 × 74.7 cm). Mead Art Museum, Amherst College, MA; bequest of Frank G. Nelson (Class of 1873). Courtesy Bridgeman Images.

p. 50 Erastus Salisbury Field, *Historical Monument of the American Republic* (1867–88), oil on canvas, 111 × 157 in. (281.9 × 398.8 cm). Michele and Donald D'Amour Museum of Fine Arts, Springfield, MA; the Morgan Wesson Memorial Collection. Photo: David Stansbury.

p. 51 Erastus Salisbury Field, *Garden of Eden* (c. 1860–65), oil on canvas mounted on board, 27 5⁄8 × 35 in. (69.9 × 88.9 cm). Michele and Donald D'Amour Museum of Fine Arts, Springfield, MA; museum purchase. Photo: John Polak.

p. 52 Samuel Jordan, *Eaton Family Memorial* (1831), oil on canvas, 21 7⁄8 × 15 1⁄2 in. (55.6 × 39.4 cm). National Gallery of Art, Washington, DC; gift of Edgar William and Bernice Chrysler Garbisch.

p. 52 Unknown American artist, *Dr. Philemon Tracy* (c. 1790), oil on paper on board on canvas, 31 1⁄8 × 28 7⁄8 in. (79.1 × 73.4 cm). National Gallery of Art, Washington, DC; gift of Edgar William and Bernice Chrysler Garbisch.

p. 53 Martin Johnson Heade, *Orchid and Hummingbirds Near a Mountain Lake* (c. 1875–90), oil on canvas, 15 3⁄16 × 20 1⁄2 in. (38.6 × 52.1 cm). Collection of Carolyn A. and Peter S. Lynch. Photo: Bob Packert / PEM.

p. 54 Thomas Hicks, *Portrait of Edward Hicks* (1838–41), oil on canvas, 27 1⁄4 × 22 1⁄8 in. (69.2 × 56.2 cm). The Colonial Williamsburg Foundation, Williamsburg, VA; museum purchase.

p. 88 Fernand Léger, *Leisure: Hommage à Louis David* (1948–49), oil on canvas, 60 1⁄2 × 72 3⁄4 in. (154 × 185 cm). Musée National d'Art Moderne, Centre Pompidou, Paris, France. © 2019 Artists Rights Society (ARS), New York / ADAGP, Paris. Courtesy Bridgeman Images.

p. 89 Edward Hicks, *Peaceable Kingdom* (c. 1816–18), oil on canvas, 18 3⁄4 × 23 1⁄2 in. (47.6 × 59.7 cm). Cleveland Museum of Art, Cleveland, OH; gift of the Hanna Fund 1945.38.

p. 89 Engraving after drawing by Richard Westall, *The Peaceable Kingdom of the Branch* (1800–15), published in *The Holy Bible*, Charles Heath, 1815, Volume II, accession #SCRB10582. Special Collections, the John D. Rockefeller Jr. Library, the Colonial Williamsburg Foundation, Williamsburg, VA.

p. 90 Edward Hicks, *The Peaceable Kingdom of the Branch* (c. 1825–30), oil on canvas, 36 1⁄4 × 44 7⁄8 in. (92.1 × 114 cm). Yale University Art Gallery, New Haven, CT.

p. 90 Henry Schenck Tanner, *A Map of North America* (1822), black-and-white line engraving with period hand color on laid paper, detail, accession #1997-5. The Colonial Williamsburg Foundation, Williamsburg, VA; museum purchase.

p. 92 Edward Hicks, *Peaceable Kingdom* (c. 1826), oil on canvas, 29 × 36 in. (73.6 × 91.4 cm).

Friends Historical Library of Swarthmore College, Swarthmore, PA. Courtesy Friends Historical Library of Swarthmore College.

p. 94 Edward Hicks, *The Peaceable Kingdom of the Branch* (1822–25), oil on canvas, 32 1⁄4 × 37 3⁄4 in. (81.9 × 95.9 cm). The Colonial Williamsburg Foundation, Williamsburg, VA; museum purchase.

p. 96 Attributed to Edward Hicks, *Portrait of a Child* (c. 1840), oil on wood, 17 3⁄8 × 14 1⁄2 in. (44.2 × 36.8 cm). National Gallery of Art, Washington, Gift of Edgar William and Bernice Chrysler Garbisch.

p. 97 Edward Hicks, *Peaceable Kingdom* (1826), oil on canvas, 32 1⁄8 × 38 1⁄8 in. (81.6 × 96.84 cm). Private collection. Photo © Christie's Images / Bridgeman Images.

p. 98 Edward Hicks, *Peaceable Kingdom* (c. 1829–30), oil on canvas, 17 1⁄2 × 23 1⁄2 in. (44.5 × 59.7 cm). Yale University Art Gallery, New Haven, CT.

p. 103 Edward Hicks, *Peaceable Kingdom* (c. 1816–18), oil on canvas, 18 3⁄4 × 23 1⁄2 in. (47.6 × 59.7 cm), detail. The Cleveland Museum of Art, Cleveland, OH; gift of the Hanna Fund 1945.38.

p. 104 Edward Hicks, *Peaceable Kingdom* (1832–34), oil on canvas, 17 1⁄4 × 23 1⁄4 in. (43.8 × 59.1 cm), detail. The Colonial Williamsburg Foundation, Williamsburg, VA; from the Abby Aldrich Rockefeller Collection; gift of David Rockefeller.

p. 106 Edward Hicks, *Peaceable Kingdom* (1829–32), oil on wood panel, 17 1⁄4 × 23 1⁄2 in. (43.8 × 59.7 cm), location unknown. Photo courtesy of Scripps College, Claremont, CA.

p. 106 Edward Hicks, *Peaceable Kingdom* (c. 1846), oil on canvas, 25 × 28 1⁄2 in. (63.5 × 72.4 cm), detail. The Fine Arts Museums of San Francisco; gift of Mr. and Mrs. John D. Rockefeller 3rd, 1993.35.14.

p. 109 Edward Hicks, *Peaceable Kingdom* (c. 1833–34), oil on canvas, 17 7⁄16 × 23 9⁄16 in. (44.3 × 59.8 cm). Brooklyn Museum, Brooklyn, NY; Dick S. Ramsay Fund, 40.340.

p. 109 Adolf Wölfli, *St. Adolf—Ring of Oberburg* (1918), pencil and colored pencil on paper, 19 1⁄2 × 27 in. (49.5 × 68.6 cm), detail. Private collection.

p. 110 Edward Hicks, *Peaceable Kingdom* (c. 1834), oil on canvas, 29 5⁄16 × 35 1⁄2 in. (74.5 × 90.1 cm). Courtesy National Gallery of Art, Washington; gift of Edgar William and Bernice Chrysler Garbisch.

p. 112 Edward Hicks, *The Peaceable Kingdom and Penn's Treaty* (1845), oil on canvas, 24 1⁄2 × 31 in. (61.6 × 78.7 cm). Yale University Art Gallery, New Haven, CT.

p. 117 Edward Hicks, *Peaceable Kingdom* (c. 1846), oil on canvas, 25 × 28 1⁄2 in. (63.5 × 72.4 cm). The Fine Arts Museums of San Francisco; gift of Mr. and Mrs. John D. Rockefeller 3rd, 1993.35.14.

p. 117 Edward Hicks, *The Peaceable Kingdom with the Leopard of Serenity* (c. 1846–48), oil on canvas, 26 × 29 1⁄2 in. (66 × 75 cm). Private collection. Courtesy Sotheby's, Inc. © 2020.

p. 118 Edward Hicks, *Peaceable Kingdom* (1845–46), oil on canvas, 24 1⁄8 × 32 1⁄8 in. (61.3 × 81.6 cm). The Phillips Collection, Washington, DC; acquired 1939.

p. 120 Edward Hicks, *The Grave of William Penn* (c. 1847–48), oil on canvas, 23 3⁄4 × 29 3⁄4 in. (60.4 × 75.5 cm). National Gallery of Art, Washington, DC; gift of Edgar William and Bernice Chrysler Garbisch.

p. 121 Edward Hicks, *The Twining Residence* (1845–47), oil on canvas, 26 1/2 × 31 9/16 in. (67.3 × 80.2 cm). The Colonial Williamsburg Foundation, Williamsburg, VA; from the Abby Aldrich Rockefeller Collection; gift of David Rockefeller.

p. 122 Edward Hicks, *The Cornell Farm* (1848), oil on canvas, 36 3/4 × 49 in. (93.3 × 124.4 cm). Courtesy National Gallery of Art, Washington; gift of Edgar William and Bernice Chrysler Garbisch.

p. 123 Edward Hicks, *Leedom Farm* (1849), oil on canvas, 40 1/8 × 49 1/16 in. (101.9 × 124.6 cm). The Colonial Williamsburg Foundation, Williamsburg, VA; museum purchase.

p. 125 Unknown American artist, *Mahantango Valley Farm* (late nineteenth century), oil on window shade, 28 × 36 5/16 in. (71.1 × 92.2 cm). Courtesy National Gallery of Art, Washington; gift of Edgar William and Bernice Chrysler Garbisch.

p. 128 Unknown artist, *Noah's Ark*, hand-colored lithograph, 8 1/4 × 12 1/2 in. (21 × 31.8 cm). Published 1838–56 by Currier & Ives, New York. Philadelphia Museum of Art, Philadelphia, PA; bequest of Lisa Norris Elkins, 1950, 1950-92-292.

p. 128 Edward Hicks, *Noah's Ark* (1846), oil on canvas, 26 5/16 × 30 3/8 in. (66.8 × 77.2 cm). Philadelphia Museum of Art, Philadelphia, PA; bequest of Lisa Norris Elkins, 1950, 1950-92-7.

p. 130 Edward Hicks, *Peaceable Kingdom* (c. 1849), oil on canvas, 24 × 30 1/4 in. (60.9 × 76.8). Private collection. Courtesy Galerie St. Etienne, New York.

p. 131 Edward Hicks, *Peaceable Kingdom* (1849), oil on canvas, 24 1/4 × 30 1/4 in. (61.6 × 76.8 cm). Private collection. Courtesy Christie's Images / Bridgeman Images.

p. 132 Edward Hicks, *The Cornell Farm* (1848), oil on canvas, 36 3/4 × 49 in. (93.3 × 124.4 cm), detail. Courtesy National Gallery of Art, Washington; gift of Edgar William and Bernice Chrysler Garbisch.

Index